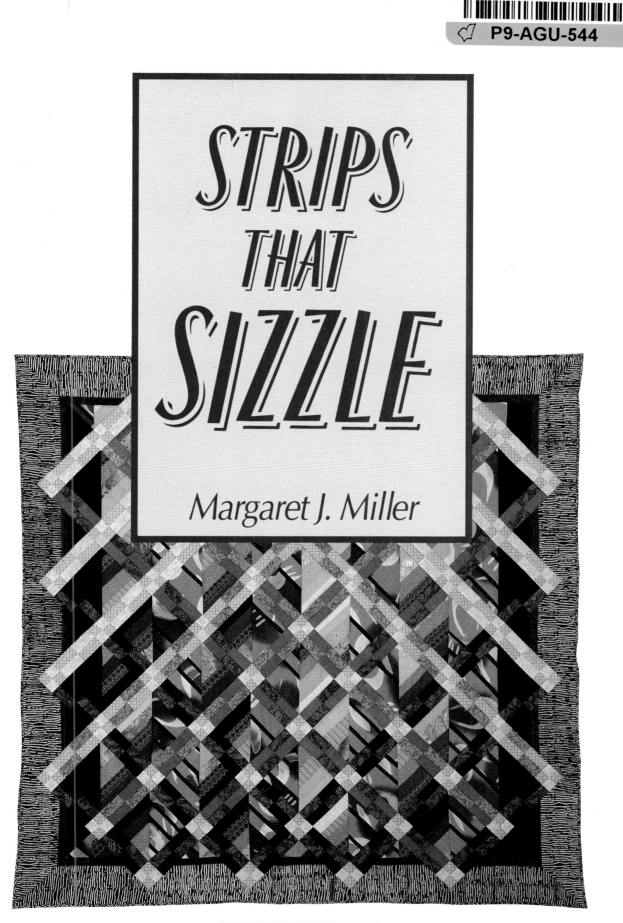

STRIPS THAT SIZZLE

Margaret J. Miller

That Patchwork Place®

2

Credits

Photography . . . . .Brian Kaplan
Illustration and Graphics . . . . .Laurel Strand
Barb Tourtillotte
Text and Cover Design . . . . .Judy Petry
Editor . . . . .Barbara Weiland
Copy Editor . . . . .Liz McGehee

Strips That Sizzle©
©1992 by Margaret J. Miller

That Patchwork Place, Inc.
PO Box 118, Bothell, WA 98041-0118

Printed in the British Crown Colony of Hong Kong
97 96 95 94 93 92   6 5 4 3 2 1

The information in this book is presented in good faith, but no warranty is given nor results guaranteed. Since That Patchwork Place, Inc., has no control over choice of materials or procedures, the company assumes no responsibility for the use of this data.

Library of Congress Cataloging-in-Publication Data

Miller, Margaret J.
     Strips that sizzle / Margaret J. Miller.
         p.   cm.
     Includes bibliographical references.
     ISBN 1-56477-009-5 :
        1. Patchwork. 2. Patchwork quilts.   I. Title.
TT835.M523   1992   92-8798
746.46—dc20   CIP

Published in the USA

Dedication

To my husband, Paul Carlyle Miller, who in so many ways has been the wind beneath my wings. . . .

Acknowledgments

My heartfelt thanks go to:

Lassie Wittman of Rochester, Washington, whose early work with strip piecing and a quilt pattern of her design were the initial seeds that eventually grew into this book;

All the students over the years who have jumped into the "Strips that Sizzle" classes with abandon, even though there was no sample quilt with which they could form preconceived ideas on what they "were supposed to be making";

All the individuals who have loaned their quilts for this book:

Ola M. Bouknight, Bellingham, Washington
Ramona Crowell, Berkeley, California
Dawn Davis, Fresno, California
Barbara J. Fowler, Newark, California
Doris Garfinkel, West Lafayette, Indiana
Susan Wells Hall, Mount Vernon, Washington
Wanda S. Hanson, Sandwich, Illinois
Karen Hauser, Yakima, Washington
Marty Hudlow, West Lafayette, Indiana
Phyllis A. Hughes, Wayne, Pennsylvania
Gloria Hunt, Alameda, California
Caryn Jennings, Poulsbo, Washington
Michelle Joanou, La Canada, California
Lucinda W. Langjahr, Bellevue, Washington
Mary Lehmann, Trumansburg, New York
Dale MacEwan, Richmond, British Columbia
Gloria Marion, Del Mar, California
Phyllis McFarland, Spokane, Washington
Nancy Kies Miller, San Carlos, California
Marla J. Morris-Kennedy, Mequon, Wisconsin
Elizabeth Noyd, Bellevue, Washington
Florence E. Peel, West Vancouver, British Columbia
Jean M. Perry, Bayport, New York
Doreen M. Rennschmid, Richmond, British Columbia
Diane Ross, Woodinville, Washington
Carol Rothrock, Nordland, Washington
Diana J. Smith, Anacortes, Washington
Beryl Sortino, Absecon, New Jersey
Vicky Van Valkenburg, Berkeley, California
Sylvia Whitesides, Lafayette, Indiana
Juanita Yeager, Louisville, Kentucky
Angie Woolman, Albany, California

The entire staff at That Patchwork Place, whose professionalism with just the right dash of humor makes publications such as this one such a joy to create and develop.

Contents

Preface

Ten years ago when I began teaching basic quiltmaking, my students often voiced their insecurities about their creative abilities by chanting "but I can't draw." Now, the phrases "but I just can't use color" or "I can't put fabrics together well" (like one of their more self-confident quilting friends) echo in quiltmaking classrooms across the country.

This book is an attempt to show not only how easy but also how exciting it can be to get over the "I can't use color" hurdle. In *Strips That Sizzle*, you will learn to think about color, not by name but by value, and to think about using color to "sprinkle light" across the quilt surface, rather than agonize about which fabric to use in any given location on the quilt surface. It's all accomplished using the simplest of quilt patterns—a square bisected by a single diagonal line.

One reason some quiltmakers agonize over choosing and placing colors in a quilt is that they try to use too few colors. When you use only three fabrics in a quilt, it is often obvious that one fabric doesn't go with one of the others. When you use thirty fabrics in a quilt, the eye blends all the fabrics together into a whole that is greater than the sum of its parts. Thus, the theme of this book is "Never use two fabrics when you can use twenty!"

This system is based on a block from a quilt designed in l979 by Lassie Wittman of Rochester, Washington. A quiltmaker and teacher known for her exploration of Seminole-strip patchwork techniques, Lassie published the pattern for the quilt (shown at left) and also included the directions for it in her book *Seminole Patchwork Patterns.* In both the pattern and the book, she included some additional placement ideas for the block in this pattern.

When I saw this quilt again in Taimi Dudley's book *Strip Patchwork*, I cut out and began assembling Lassie's quilt, which was based on precisely cut strips of particular color arrangements. However, I soon became so intrigued by the numerous designs I could produce with the block when I cut strips of random width, that the original quilt project remains in pieces to this day.

The ideas for exploring fabric values generated by that unfinished project led to the Strips That Sizzle series of quilts, two of which were included in Quilt National exhibitions. I then began to teach workshops in this design technique; the work of many of the nearly five hundred students who took those classes appears in the pages of this book.

Crossroads to Seminole by Lassie Wittman, 1979, Rochester, Washington, 104" x 114".

Introduction

This is not meant to be a pattern book, but rather a book of ideas—of directions you can take to explore how to "sprinkle light" across the quilt surface. Though it seems that certain formulas are being described throughout, I encourage you to use these as jumping-off places for quilts, not as prescriptions for a "perfect" quilt. There are many more suggested layouts for quilts in this book than are illustrated in the color mock-ups or photos of finished quilts. As you try the layouts with your own blocks, be sure to keep a camera handy to photograph them as you go; you may design hundreds of quilt surfaces as you explore the color adventures in these pages. Another reason to photograph each arrangement you put up on the wall is that you may arrive at a wonderful quilt design, move two or three blocks, and then not be able to get back to that wonderful design again without a snapshot to guide you!

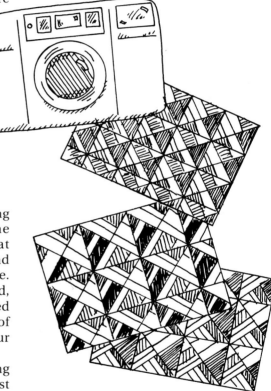

How to Use This Book

The book's primary chapters concern: 1) choosing fabrics, focusing on value rather than color name; 2) the mechanics of making the Strips That Sizzle block; 3) sample layouts with this block that create numerous and surprising design motifs on the quilt surface; and 4) design diversions, both within the block and across the pieced surface. In addition, special uses of sashing strips and borders are presented, followed by some design challenges for you in the form of preplanned projects to try; these projects are designed to help you use a number of the concepts presented in the book to "reach for the unexpected" in your own Strips That Sizzle quilts.

First, peruse the entire book to get an overview of the block-making process as well as the scope of design possibilities. Next, choose at least six values (dark to light) in each of two color families and make a set of at least thirty 6" Strips That Sizzle blocks. These blocks can be made quickly, following the basic directions on page 12. Then, rearrange these basic blocks according to various exercises throughout the chapter "Making Magic with Strips That Sizzle Blocks," beginning on page 17.

Work on a vertical design surface (page 8), recording any wonderful quilt designs that may emerge with a snapshot. If you photograph every arrangement you create on your design wall, when you turn the subsequent photographs upside down or sideways, you may find that you have designed a magnificent quilt without even knowing it!

Once you have played with some basic arrangements of your blocks, you will be ready to expand your fabric choices and perhaps combine various motifs in a single quilt surface.

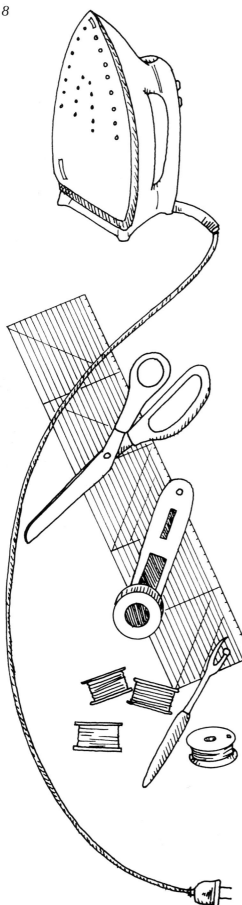

Supplies

Cutting Tools

Large-wheel rotary cutter

Cutting surface for rotary cutter. The bigger, the better, it should be at least wide enough to rotary cut across the width of the fabric folded selvage to selvage. Mine is 23" x 35".

Acrylic ruler for rotary cutting, at least 6" x 24". A 6" square is handy and a 12" or 15" square with multiple-size squares marked on it is helpful as you make Strips That Sizzle blocks of various sizes.

Sewing Tools

Sewing machine in good running condition, recently cleaned and oiled

Five or six bobbins filled with appropriate thread

Good steam iron and pressing surface

Seam ripper!

Scissors or thread-snipper

Designing Tools

Good lighting

Vertical design surface. This is essential to good quilt design and color analysis. It could consist of:

1. 4' x 8' panel(s) of Celotex or soundboard, covered with flannel fabric;
2. lengths of Pellon fleece stretched on a wall or otherwise suspended on a vertical surface.

Your Strips That Sizzle blocks will "stick" to the fuzzy surfaces of these fabrics so you can stand back to analyze them in relation to the entire design.

Color Wheel. Even an inexpensive color wheel can be an invaluable tool when choosing color combinations for quilts. References to the color wheel will be made from time to time throughout this book.

Reducing or distancing devices. This might be a reducing glass (just the opposite of a magnifying glass and available in many quilt shops

or office supply stores), or you can use binoculars and look through the "wrong end." Some quiltmakers buy the "peephole" that is usually inserted in a front door as a security viewing device for distancing themselves from the quilt in progress.

The farther away you can stand from a vertical quilt in progress, the better you can analyze its overall color and design. Reducing tools are especially helpful if you have a very small space in which to work.

Other tools that aid in the design-evaluation process are a mirror and a camera. If you turn your back on the design board and look at the design through a mirror, sometimes glaring design or color problems become immediately evident. A camera does not distance you from your design as much as a reducing glass does, but at least, looking at your quilt through the viewfinder of a camera masks out the other visual stimuli in the room, allowing you to focus on the quilt alone.

Camera (with flash capability) to photograph the various Strips That Sizzle layouts that you may discover and to analyze and compare them at a later time. Snapshots taken of a quilt in progress often lead to many other quilt ideas—and thus a "working series" evolves.

Template-making materials. You will need a few simple templates for some of the borders that appear in this book. (See Appendix B.) For such templates, I recommend the following supplies:

Graph paper. I use a cross-section pad with eight squares per inch for all my quilt-design and template work.

Poster board. Purchase white or a light color in large-sheet size (22" x 28"). The inexpensive dime-store variety is just fine for templates.

Spray adhesive or rubber cement

Scissors or rotary cutter for paper. I recycle my dull blades in a separate rotary cutter that I use for paper and poster board only.

Idea Book. The Strips That Sizzle block is so versatile and the system for using it so simple that you may find yourself getting ideas for quilts faster than you can process them! I keep a spiral-bound notebook handy for recording color ideas in the form of words, sketches, or quick charts, using copies of the work sheets found in Appendix A (page 103). Ideas are merely recorded in this notebook; they may later be organized in a three-ring binder. This binder might also include pages with fabric swatches to record value choices for completed and future quilts.

Time to let the design evolve. Observe your arrangements of Strips That Sizzle blocks on the wall at various times of the day and from different angles. Sometimes, you will come around the corner and see something in the quilt design from a new angle that you never saw during the hours of working with it "up close and personal."

Remember, *speed* is not the goal; *delight* in the *adventure* of discovering new designs and new ways you can sprinkle light over the pieced surface is the reward for playing with the Strips That Sizzle blocks.

Fabrics

Strips That Sizzle blocks begin with many strips of fabric that have been cut with a rotary cutter, using an acrylic ruler as a guide; the strips are then sewn together, using a ¼"-wide seam allowance. Good-quality, finely woven (medium to high thread count), plain-weave fabrics are recommended. Cotton or cotton/polyester blends are best. Fabrics made of all polyester, or other fibers or weaves, are not recommended.

Color Choices

The block we will use to make Strips That Sizzle quilts is one of the simplest: a square bisected by one diagonal line, corner to corner. The magic of this block is that the two triangles thus formed are made not of a single fabric in each, but of many fabrics.

Beginning quiltmakers often agonize over the fabric choices for their quilts. They may carefully choose fabrics that have been "dyed to match" by manufacturers, or they may choose only two or three fabrics for their first quilt. This restricts them to too few fabrics. Remember, the theme of this book is "never use two fabrics when you can use twenty."

When you restrict yourself to three or four or even six fabrics in a quilt, it may be obvious that one of those fabrics "doesn't quite go" with one of the others. If you use many fabrics, on the other hand, the eye tends to blend all the fabrics together, and no one fabric stands out as a "misfit."

Let me hasten to add that there are some quilts for which only two or three fabrics are appropriate, and such choices work well, but for Strips That Sizzle quilts, you will be better off choosing many fabrics rather than fewer.

You will make your basic set of Strips That Sizzle blocks from only two color families. Once you have made this set of blocks and performed some of the manipulations in "Making Magic with Strips That Sizzle Blocks" (page 17), you may want to add more fabrics, perhaps leave out one or two of the original group, or add another color family. But to begin to work with the Strips That Sizzle blocks, restrict yourself to two color families. For best results, choose two color families that are opposite each other on the color wheel (complementary colors).

Value Choices

The value of a color is its lightness or darkness. The values of the color orange, for example, might range from the palest of peach tones to apricot, orange, red-orange, to red-brown, through the rusts, all the way to rusty loam and black-brown. One of the challenges facing emerging quiltmakers is to incorporate more values into their quilts—to go "all the way up to the lights" and "all the way down to the darks." For many quiltmakers it is actually difficult to buy fabrics in the light or light-medium value range. Many smaller shops cannot stock a wide range of them, and some seasons manufacturers produce fabrics in mostly medium to dark values, with very few in the lighter values.

Take a moment now and examine the fabric in your collection. Do you have a good range of light, medium, and dark values?

When you are choosing fabrics by value, it is important to evaluate them from a distance, not just close up; also, arrange fabrics so that approximately the same amount of each fabric is visible. Fan out the fabrics, arranging the values from lightest to darkest. In a fabric store, stack bolts of fabric from lightest to darkest; then move to the other side of the store to look at them.

Some people like to look at the stacked fabrics through a piece of red or green acrylic or through a red or green plastic "report cover." I find it just as easy to squint at the fabrics or to view them in lowered light. Late afternoon natural light is good, or turn out most of the lights in the room. You will see color less and the value more.

In the basic set of blocks you make to get the feel for this quilt design system, you will choose five or six values, ranging from very light to very dark, in each of two color families. In this process, try to get the same strength of values in each color family; for example, be sure that your darkest values are of equal strength.

Making the Basic Set of Blocks

Do not agonize over the first set of fabrics you choose; the idea is that you will make a basic set of blocks and play with various arrangements of them to see what they can do. Then, you will have a better idea of what you *really* want to sew together. You may want to add lights or darks, or eliminate one of the fabrics you chose in the original lineup.

You may also find that, when the fabrics are cut into strips, they may take on a slightly different value in your lineup; this is to be expected, especially if this is the first time you have tried to work with numerous values in the same quilt. If it is very difficult to decide whether Fabric A is darker or lighter than Fabric B, these two fabrics will probably be interchangeable in your Strips That Sizzle block. *Don't agonize—jump in and sew them together!*

Cutting the Strips for the Basic Set of Blocks

First, prepare strips of fabric in each of the two color families you have chosen. Begin with ½ yard of fabric for each of at least five or six values (light to dark) in each of two color families. For example, you might have five half-yard cuts of reds (light to dark) and five half-yard cuts of greens, for a total of five yards of fabric.

One of the secrets to using the Strips That Sizzle design system successfully is to incorporate as much variety from block to block as possible. To do this, you will be using a half-width of fabric, even though you will be cutting a full width (selvage to selvage) at a time. Before cutting the strips, fold the fabric selvage to selvage, then cut along the fold with scissors.

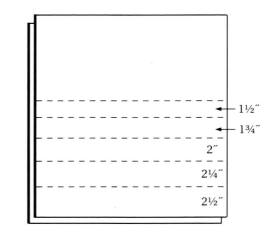

Next, place the folded and slit fabric on an appropriate cutting surface and, using an acrylic ruler and rotary cutter, cut one strip in each of the following widths:

2½"   2¼"   2"   1¾"   1½"

You may find that you can cut two or three doubled fabrics at once, as long as you have a sharp rotary blade in your cutter.

If you have a print in this first group of fabrics that could go with either color family, assign it to *one or the other* family. Do not sew strips of it into both color families.

Organizing Your Strips

To make the basic Strips That Sizzle block, you will need easy access to various fabric widths and various values for each grouping that you sew together. It is best to keep all your strips at arm's reach while seated at your machine.

Set up a spare ironing board (or a card table or TV trays) to the left of your sewing machine and arrange the loose strips by color family and value on that surface. As you work with them, the strips may end up in a jumbled pile and need to be straightened partway through the assembly process; however, it is easier to pick strip widths at random, and thus build more variety into your set of blocks, when the strips are in disarray.

For storing leftover strips, use several multiple pants hangers. You can store many fabrics in a small space and keep the colors of the strips visible.

Sewing the Strips and Cutting the Blocks

The menu of motifs that follows this section provides some striking three-dimensional effects, which are possible only if you follow certain guidelines to make the blocks. After making the basic set of blocks and trying these exercises, you may purposely "break" the rules; however, in order to see how versatile this design system is, follow the steps below to make all your basic blocks.

For the sample blocks, use a 6" acrylic template. You may have a 6½" square template in your tool collection, which is also acceptable. Whichever you begin using, use it throughout the process so that all your blocks will be the same size. You will be making thirty blocks for your basic set.

1. In each color family, sew a grouping of strips together with ¼"-wide seams. Begin with the darkest value at one edge of the grouping and add strips in successively lighter values. Sew enough strips together so that you can cut a 6" square from them. You will need to sew at least four strips together, sometimes five, in order to do this.

LIGHTEST
LIGHTER
LIGHTER
LIGHTER
DARKEST

As you select different combinations of strips to sew together in each color family, mix up the widths of strips you choose as you go from darker to lighter values; you are not sewing wider to narrower, only darker to lighter.

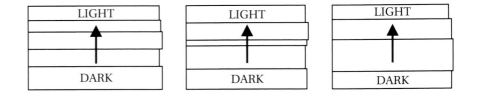

2. To make your basic set of thirty blocks, sew together at least five groupings of strips in each color family. Six is better, for more variety.

   Remember: Each strip grouping will be slightly different fabric widths and fabric combinations, but all will go from dark to light across the strip grouping. Don't start all strip groupings with the same dark fabric or end with the same light fabric. Several groupings may start with the same dark, or end with the same light, but don't start and end *all* groupings with the same fabrics.

3. Press seams in the strip groupings toward the darkest strips. Press from the wrong side first, then from the right side, making sure there is no "bubbling" or "pleating" at the seam line.

4. Take one grouping of strips from each color family and place them on the table, *right sides together.* Make a note of *which color is "against the table."* It is important that this color *always* be in this position. In other words, if you are working with reds and blues, don't cut some blocks with reds against the table and some with blues against the table.

   Be sure that the "*darks are in your lap.*" In other words, the darkest values are closest to you in both color families. Don't cut some blocks with the "darks in your lap" and some with the "lights in your lap."

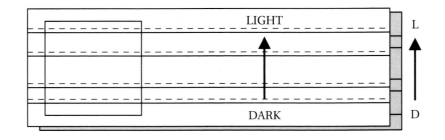

5. Place a 6" acrylic square on top of these groupings; cut around the square with a rotary cutter.

6. Make a diagonal cut in each stack of squares, corner to corner. *Before making this cut,* check your set of fabric squares again to make sure that you have right sides together, the proper color against the table,

and darks in your lap. Make the corner-to-corner cut, cutting in the same direction *every time.* In other words, don't make some diagonal cuts right to left and others left to right. You will have two sets of triangle pairs in a ready-to-sew position.

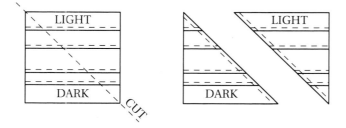

7. Using a ¼"-wide seam allowance, sew each triangle pair together along the diagonal edge. Press. For less bulk in joining the blocks, press all seams toward the same color family.

When you cut and sew triangle pairs from a set of squares, you actually get two blocks. One has the darkest values along one edge; the companion block has the lightest values along one edge.

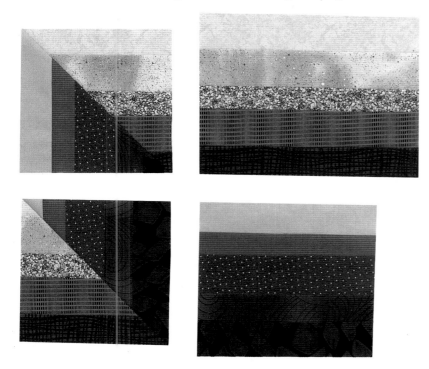

Remember that the key to this quilt design system is to build in as much variety as possible. Therefore, instead of cutting out your next square from the same combination of strip groupings, take the top strip layer off the combination you have just cut and replace it with another strip grouping from the same color family. Cut another square from this new combination, using the guidelines above. Continue cutting squares in this fashion, always cutting them from a different "fabric sandwich" each time.

To help you remember the cutting guidelines, cut out your first block, make the diagonal cut, and move the triangle pairs to one side of your cutting surface without sewing the diagonal seam. This will remind you which color should be against the table and in which direction every diagonal cut should be made.

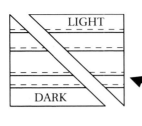

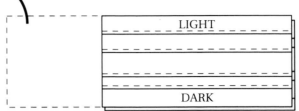

As you cut and sew successive blocks, stop occasionally to make sure you are cutting and sewing the blocks consistently. To check this, place all your blocks on the design wall or on the table "on point" so that all the longest strips form the letter "V." Line up all diagonal seams. When you do this, color family A should be to the left of the diagonal seam, and color family B should be to the right of that seam. If you discover a situation like that shown on the right, below, where the color families "jump" the diagonal seam, you have sewn those blocks inconsistently with the other blocks. Perhaps you had the wrong color against the table, or darks were not in your lap when you cut the diagonal, or you cut the diagonal in a different direction. Do not destroy these "inconsistent" blocks; put a pin in them and set them aside for now.

A   B

Making Magic with Strips That Sizzle Blocks

A Menu of Motifs

You will soon discover that there are literally hundreds of ways that the Strips That Sizzle blocks can be combined to create a pieced quilt surface; only a small portion of those design strategies are presented here. In the exercises below, you will see how your blocks can form various patterns of light and dark, as well as various specific motifs, like stars, columns, or pinwheels, for example. These design "nuggets" can later be combined and expanded into full-size quilts or wall hangings.

In successive chapters, we will explore variations on the themes presented in this section.

Be sure to take a snapshot of your blocks in each of the design exercises below. Sometimes, you can see more in a snapshot of a group of blocks than you can see standing right in front of them, even when you view them through a reducing glass. Moreover, you may stumble onto some wonderful block arrangements in the process of doing these exercises, to which you will want to return later to develop into a whole quilt.

Snapshots are also great design tools in that you can take a snapshot of a given design exercise and turn it upside down, sideways, or "on point" to see what your arrangement looks like from a different vantage point, without having to rearrange the actual blocks. Whenever you design quilts on a vertical surface, even if you are pleased with the results, you may find that the quilt you designed is smashing if viewed "upside down!"

When you put your blocks up on the design wall, be sure to place them edge to edge with no wall showing between them so it will be easier to visualize these groupings as "real quilts."

Warning: Your blocks may not look terrific in every exercise! The values you have chosen to work with in this first set of blocks are not guaranteed to be the best combination of fabrics for these blocks! The whole point of doing these exercises is to see what your fabrics look like in this context. By doing the exercises, you will discover what you *really* want to sew together! Perhaps you will discover that you do not have enough light values, or you might have much darker values in one color family than in the other. Perhaps there is a fabric that doesn't work in these blocks. You may decide to leave it out in the rest of the blocks you sew together.

Regardless of the good or "less thrilling" results you get with your blocks, remember that this is an *additive* process; after completing the exercises, you will be making more blocks and adding them to this basic set; you won't be pitching these blocks out and starting over. When you use this approach, the less effective blocks become background for the blocks that sing the song you want them to sing. For example, if you have not used enough light values in your blocks, when you make more blocks that do bring light into the surface, the original set becomes background for the drama that the light blocks bring to the quilt.

Also, you have a very limited number of blocks with which to work

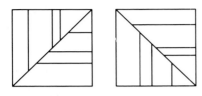

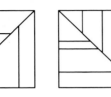

as you try these exercises. You may discover that the same design exercise will look very different in a full-size quilt than it does with only the basic thirty blocks you are using to get started.

What makes the magic in the Strips That Sizzle system are the three dynamic *block variables* that interact in the design process:

1. The block is asymmetrical.
2. There are light blocks and dark blocks.
3. Within each block, there is a movement of values from light to dark.

The block is asymmetrical because it looks different, depending on "which side is up," as seen in the illustrations at left.

Different combinations of asymmetrical blocks yield dissimilar *design categories*, depending on whether the design consists of

1. a single block
2. a block and one or more rotated versions of it
3. a block and one or more mirror images

Since there are "light blocks" (blocks with the light values along one edge) and "dark blocks" (blocks with the dark values along one edge), various light patterns can be applied to the motifs derived in the three design categories above. The *light patterns* we will consider are the following:

1. all lights together or all darks together
2. horizontal and vertical stripes
3. checkerboards (single block, 2 by 2, 3 by 3, or more blocks as "checkers")
4. diagonals (single, double, or triple rows of blocks)
5. crossed diagonals (single, double, or multiple rows of blocks)
6. radiating or concentric designs
7. offset designs

Each of the light strategies listed above can be applied to each of the hundreds of block combinations in design categories 1–3, above. Some light-strategy and motif combinations are more successful than others in any given block arrangement. We will not be presenting every light strategy with every block arrangement, *but you are encouraged to do so with your blocks.*

Likewise, some block combinations and light strategies are more successful in some groupings of fabrics than in others. You might try these various combinations with a small group of quilting friends, and you will learn much about how fabrics go together in quilts. Don't forget to take a color snapshot of each of the block arrangements you try.

You may want to make some large numbers on index cards to photograph along with your arrangement; these numbers may refer to notes or sketches of the layout in your idea book, or perhaps they refer to the pages in this book on which the photographed layout appears.

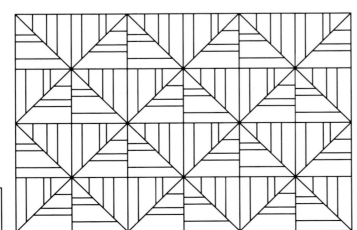

25

The final design magic happens when you take these snapshots and study the block arrangements, looking at them right side up, upside down, from both sides, and especially "on point," or from each of the four corners.

As previously stated, we will be making block arrangements based on "light" blocks and "dark" blocks. Look at the longest strips of any given block to determine its category. If the longest strips in the block are your darkest values, it is a "dark" block; if the longest strips are your lightest values, it is a "light" block. In the charts that follow, the light and dark blocks are indicated as shown at right. Note that the letter appears in the corner of the block where the long strips come together; the diagonal line is the diagonal seam in the block. Some of the following block arrangements are shown in both a chart and a color mock-up; others are shown only in a chart. Use your blocks to try the arrangements with both chart and mock-up first, to help you become accustomed to reading the charts.

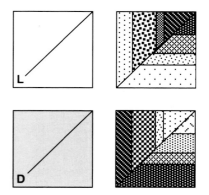

The Single Block

Place all your blocks on the wall in the same orientation, so that the long strips form the letter "L."

All Lights Together or All Darks Together

The first light strategy is to put all your light blocks together (three rows of five blocks), then all your dark blocks together (again, three rows of five blocks).

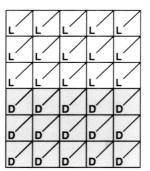

In this first exercise, you get a feeling for the fabrics you have combined. You may get some surprises the first time you put your blocks up on the wall and stand back from them. As you examine the blocks, answer the following questions: Do you have a different impression of your fabrics now than you did when they were merely groupings of strips sewn together in color families? Are some fabrics, which were obvious as you were sewing them, now not obvious at all? Are you discovering that you didn't go all the way down to the darks in the values you chose, or all the way up to the lights? Did you do so in one color family, but not in the other?

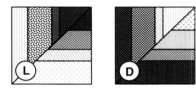

If you did not go very dark and very light in your fabric selections, you may find it difficult to work with this first set of blocks because you can't tell which is a "light" block and which is a "dark" one. If this is true for your blocks, go through and label them accordingly, using a small, self-adhesive label that will not interfere with the view of the block. (If you use self-adhesive labels, do not iron the block during this process!)

Look at the types of fabrics you used and answer these questions: Did you choose print designs that are very similar in size? If so, you may discover that you have a very textured, but very even surface. Did you select all print designs of such a small size that they look like solid-colored fabrics from a distance? Did you incorporate one or two very large print designs, which now tend to become a focus (or perhaps a distraction) for the pieced surface?

Look at the proportion of solid-colored fabrics to printed fabrics. Do they now form a cohesive surface, or do you want to change the proportion in the blocks you continue to make?

Look at the transition of dark to light values in each color family. Is it a smooth, gradual value transition or is it choppy?

Note: This does *not* mean that "smooth is good" and "choppy is bad." It merely means that these are two different kinds of value transitions you may use in your blocks. For example, let's say you are using reds and blues in this first set of Strips That Sizzle blocks. You have a really smooth transition of dark to light in the red half of the blocks, but a choppy one in the blue half, going from your darkest blue to a medium blue rather than from dark to dark-medium, then gradually through medium, light-medium, and light. For a smoother transition in the blue half of the blocks, cut at least two more blue fabrics in a dark-medium value and incorporate those new strips into subsequent groupings.

Look at the darkest darks and the lightest lights in each of your color families. Are they both the same strength, or do you have a much stronger dark value in one color family than in the other?

When you put all your dark blocks together, the visual illusion is that you are looking at a bank of post-office boxes, and there is a "light at the end of the tunnel." When you look at all your light blocks together, it looks like "the view from the other side," or a shaft of light falling slightly in front of the post-office boxes, with the light catching just the lip of the openings.

One of your options after this exercise is to make two quilts out of the groupings of blocks you made, using all the dark blocks in one quilt and all the light blocks in the other.

Horizontal and Vertical Stripes

Place your light and dark blocks in horizontal rows as in the chart to the right. Ask yourself the same questions you did in the first light strategy (page 20).

If you always "started with the same dark" and "ended with the same light" when you were sewing your strips together, you will see strong dark and light lines across the quilt surface. This can be a strong design element or a visual distraction, depending upon your specific fabrics. If you always started with the same dark, for example, the dark line across the surface may be a solid bold line, or perhaps a line of varied width, depending upon the width of the strip you sewed and the actual location of the block you cut in the strip grouping.

Horizontal rows of light and dark blocks, turned on point, is the light strategy used by Wanda Hanson in her quilt "Fractured Pansies." Note the strength of the dark and light diagonal lines that go from lower left to upper right. Then, notice the diagonal lines formed by the longest block strips going in the other direction; though these lines are in the same color family, their effect is much more diluted because they are formed by alternating light and dark blocks, rather than all lights or all darks. This element of alternating values puts sparkle into the quilt.

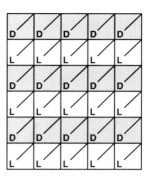

Fractured Pansies by Wanda S. Hanson, 1991, Sandwich, Illinois, 54" x 42". The quiltmaker combined newly available yellows and golds with purples she had collected to create this dazzling design.

You might try other kinds of stripes; remember to photograph each one with its appropriate index-card number. You may not have enough blocks to do the following charts completely; however, you can get an idea of how your blocks might work in these stripe combinations.

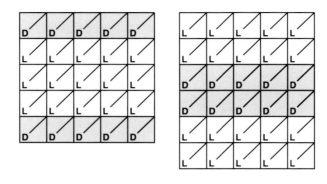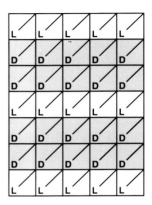

Which is your favorite stripe pattern with your current blocks? Make a note of this in your idea book.

Place your light and dark blocks in vertical rows as shown below. You may think that you can just turn the snapshots of the previous exercises on their sides; but remember, your blocks will no longer be in the same orientation. The longest strips will not form the letter "L."

Here are some more vertical striping patterns to try with your blocks:

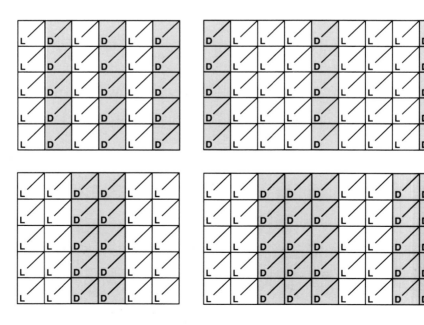

In this and every other block combination and light-strategy exercise that follows, notice the same aspects of your fabric selections you did in the first exercise when you grouped all lights together and all darks together.

Checkerboards

With the long strips of your blocks still forming the letter "L," make a one-by-one checkerboard, as shown below.

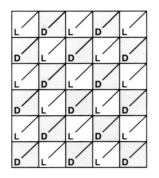

This arrangement often gives the quilt a "shimmery" surface because all of the dark blocks are completely surrounded by light ones, and vice versa. The contrast makes the most of the lights and darks.

This arrangement will also indicate something about your fabric selection. If you went "all the way up to the lights" and "all the way down to the darks" in some blocks and not in others, the latter group will tend to form a background area for the areas of greatest contrast, which will become the focal point of your quilt.

The quilt surface takes on a different look if the checkerboard is expanded to include larger groupings of blocks. Try your blocks in the arrangements below.

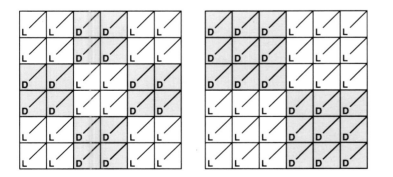

Note that these arrangements concentrate your lights and your darks into a more obvious checkerboard pattern.

Take several photographs of your blocks in each of these multiple-block checkerboard arrangements, always standing the same distance away from your design board so that all of the photographed blocks will be approximately the same size. We will cut up these photographs in the "Rotation" exercises, beginning on page 39.

Diagonals

If you examine a one-by-one checkerboard on the diagonal, you will see that it is an arrangement of alternating single diagonal rows of darks and lights. Look at the first illustration in the checkerboard exercises, on page 23.

You can make the diagonal light pattern more obvious if you arrange multiple rows of blocks of the same value along the diagonal. Note that the wider the "swath of light," the easier it is to identify the pattern across the quilt surface.

Try these additional diagonal arrangements with your blocks.

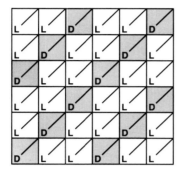 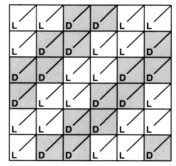 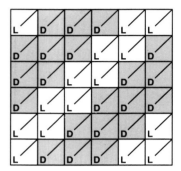

Another possibility is to "zigzag" your diagonal rows across the quilt surface. As you can see in the examples below, this pattern is more effective with multiple rows of blocks rather than single ones. The large pattern shown below has more blocks than you have in your basic set, but you should be able to tell with your thirty basic blocks whether this is a viable plan to pursue with your chosen fabrics.

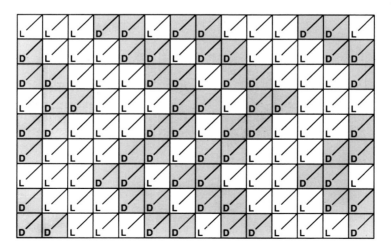 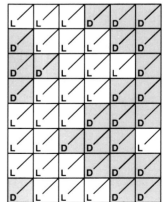

Crossed Diagonals

The same principles apply here as with diagonal arrangements: the more blocks together, the easier it is to see the pattern on the quilt surface. The patterns are also easier to see if you have gone "all the way up to the lights" and "all the way down to the darks."

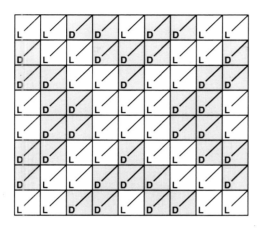

Use your blocks to try the arrangements shown below.

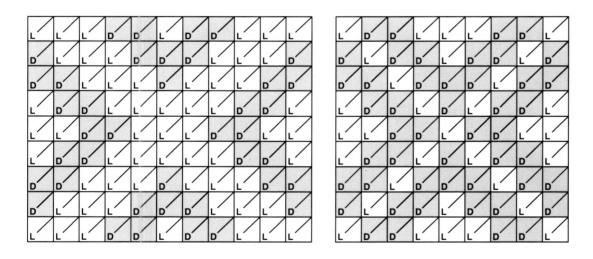

Radiating Designs

These designs are based on concentric arrangements of blocks, that is, one or more in the center, surrounded by rings of a single row or multiple rows of blocks.

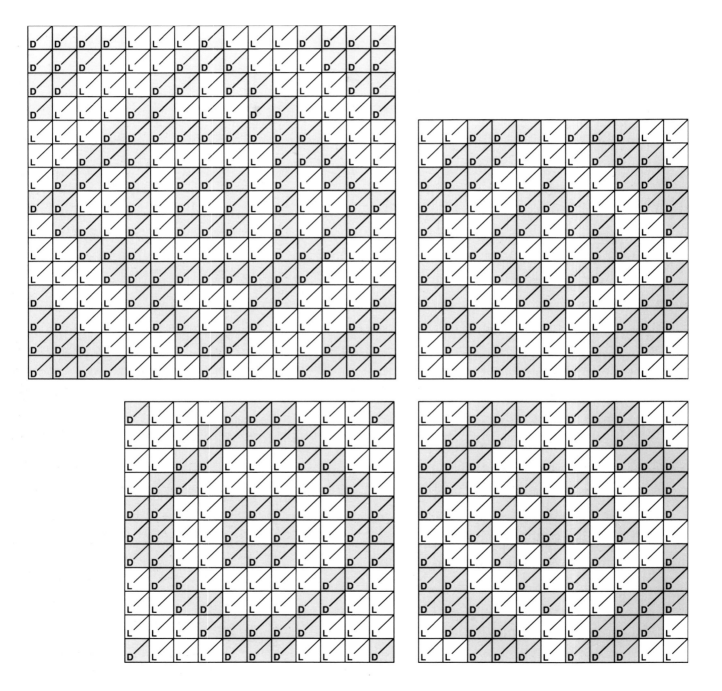

These radiating designs are particularly dramatic when turned "on point," so be sure to study the snapshots you take of these arrangements by turning them on point at all four corners. Each time you rotate the photo, you'll get a different view.

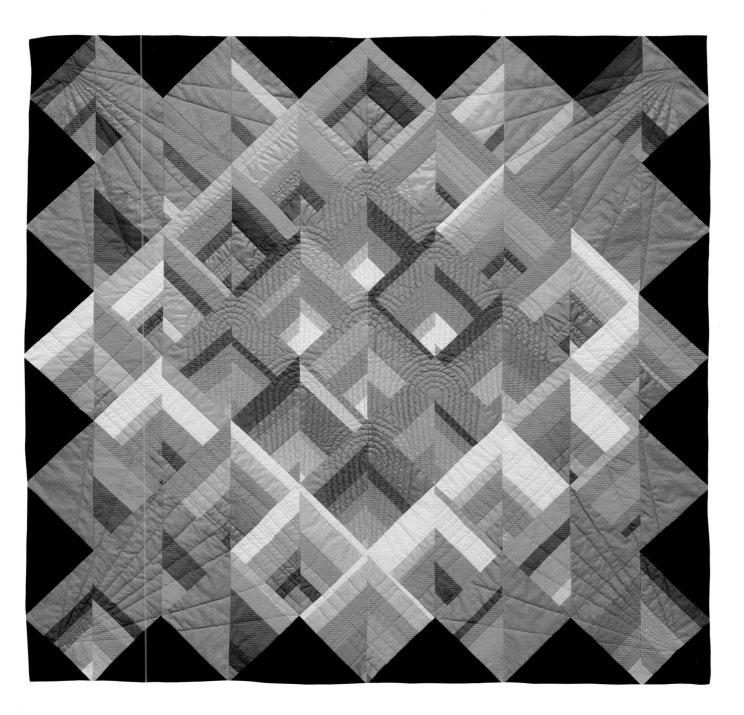

The center of my quilt "Melon Patch" was based on just such a block arrangement. There are nine dark blocks in the center, surrounded by a ring of light blocks. The blocks in the corners are not all strip-pieced; some were made by combining a strip grouping with a solid-colored fabric rather than two strip groupings to make the original blocks. Also, both color families were used in every grouping of strips; these techniques are explained in greater detail in the "Design Diversions" chapter, beginning on page 74.

Melon Patch by Margaret J. Miller, 1982, San Marcos, California, 55" x 55". This quilt was part of the 1985 Quilt National Exhibition in Athens, Ohio.

Offset Designs

This light-pattern strategy is not applicable in all block arrangements but could be effective in striped sections and checkerboards. For example, if you were to offset some of your stripe arrangements, you would get checkerboards; the offsetting could be done evenly or unevenly, as in the diagrams below.

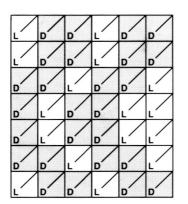 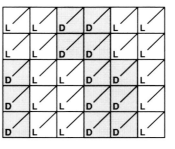 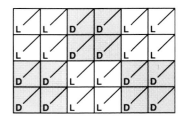

The checkerboard patterns likewise could be offset. Using your blocks, try the arrangements below.

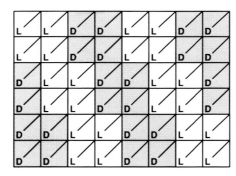 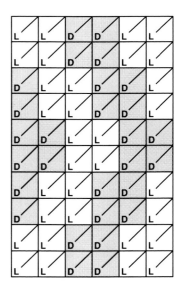

Single Block and One Rotation

In the section above, all the blocks were oriented identically so that the long strips form the letter "L." From now on, we will combine that block with blocks of a different orientation (rotated blocks or mirror-image blocks).

We will not apply all of the light strategies explained above under "The Single Block" to all the motifs that follow, *but I encourage you to do so with your blocks.*

Rotation by Row

Place a horizontal row of five light blocks in the original orientation on your board. Next, place a row of dark blocks, but rotate the blocks 180°. (The diagonal seams will be parallel to each other.)

Repeat this two-row pattern with the remaining blocks. Depending on your particular fabrics, you may see the illusion of one-color parallelograms "floating" on the other color background, or perhaps little cubicles formed by vertical walls of one color coming forward from a dark background of the other color.

Now, try some other light strategies with this rotation pattern.

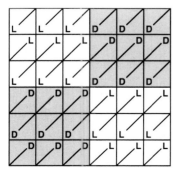
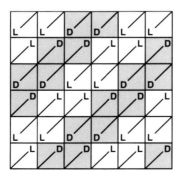

For another version of this rotation, remove the even-numbered rows and reposition the blocks in those rows as shown below.

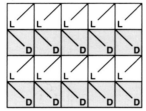

In this variation, you may see "flying geese" formed with one color family "flying" in one direction; but if you turn away and look at the blocks from a new perspective, the "geese" of the other family may become obvious.

This variation will show you immediately if you always started with the same dark or ended with the same light; these values will tend to form "drawing lines" across the surface. Sometimes, the lines thus formed distract in a negative way from the movement of the values around them. It might be more pleasing to have a variation, either in width of strip or by varying the fabrics chosen, to break up this strong visual line so it becomes better incorporated into the shapes around it.

Juanita Yeager used this design strategy, viewed from its side, in her quilt "Dawn of Tonal Enlightenment" (page 31). Note that Juanita's lightest values are much stronger than her darkest values; also, if she had ended each purple strip grouping with the same light, the resultant vertical lines on the surface would have destroyed the delicacy and mystery of this piece.

Dawn of Tonal Enlightenment by Juanita G. Yeager, 1989, Louisville, Kentucky, 68" x 68". Movement of values in the border and innovative block placement in this quilt help camouflage where the blocks stop and the border begins.

Rotation by Block

Place a column of five light blocks in the original orientation (long strips form the letter "L"). To the right of that column, place a vertical row of dark blocks, rotated as shown below. Repeat this sequence for six columns.

In reality, this is a block and its mirror image combined in the same pieced surface.

At first glance, this seems to be the "flying geese" rotation described on page 30, just turned on its side. But, look again. The "geese," which are now "little mountains," are made up of one triangle from each color family.

Try the following light strategies in this design with your own blocks. Notice what a different feeling each conveys, even though they are all the same motif.

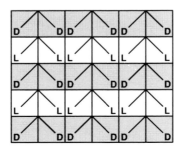

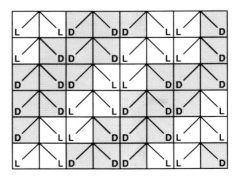

Four-Way Rotations

In the following rotations, we will be exploring the motifs formed when we rotate a block from its four corners; first letter the corners of the block A, B, C, and D, as in the diagram below.

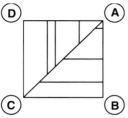

If you put all "A's" to the center, you get what looks like a pinwheel with an open box behind it.

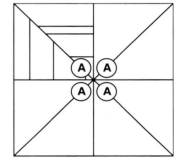

If you put four light blocks together, it looks like there is a light box behind the pinwheel, shining through the tips of the pinwheel blades. If you put four dark blocks together, you still see the pinwheel, but it looks like a shadow is hitting the edges of the pinwheel blades. In addition, there is often an intriguing asymmetrical star in the center of the blocks.

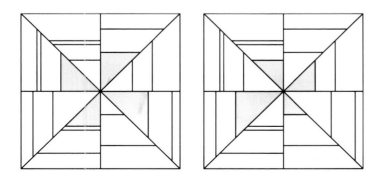

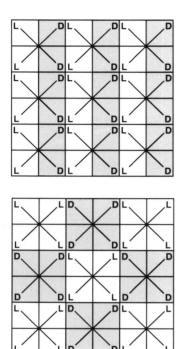

Try your blocks in the light strategies shown at left.

Doris Garfinkel's quilt "Xel-Há," below, was designed with the pattern shown at left (bottom), but placed on point with the light and dark rotations creating the checkerboard. Notice how the quilt progresses from light to dark, yet maintains the checkerboard effect throughout.

Xel-Há by Doris Garfinkel, 1991, West Lafayette, Indiana, 62" x 101". This quilt was inspired by a visit to Mayan ruins (particularly the pyramid of Kukulcan) and the fish at Xel-Há, the world's largest natural aquarium.

The stark light and dark fabrics used to fill in the area between the blocks and the border accentuate aspects of the blocks within.

The "offset" light strategy, shown below, is also a good arrangement.

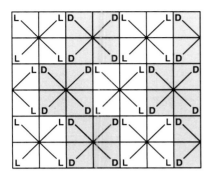 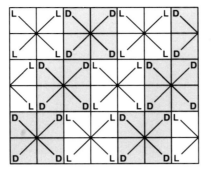

Be sure to look at photographs of these various arrangements from different vantage points, since you may discover entirely new plans for quilts in the process. For example, if we take the offset light strategy from the illustration (above, right) and turn it on its side, we still see offset pinwheels, but the design starts "midblock" instead of with a complete pinwheel. This vantage point makes other aspects of the pattern more obvious; now it looks like vertical alternating rows of diamonds and pinwheels (at right).

Look at the different patterns that emerge when you apply the following two light strategies to this block arrangement.

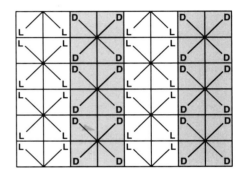

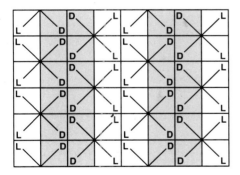 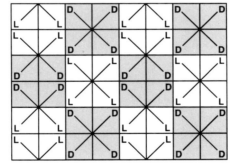

If we put "Cs to the center," we find the longest strips forming crosses where the four blocks meet. If you have a narrower range of light to dark in your blocks, this will make the most of the lights and darks you have included, because it will bring the longest strips in these values together.

 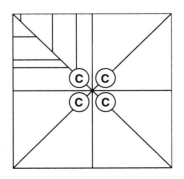

Now try the following light strategies, using the "Cs to the center" rotation.

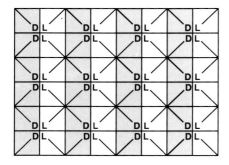 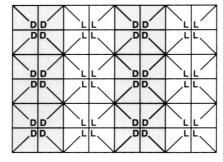 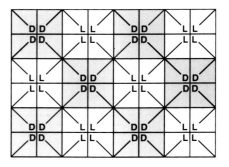

The last of these light strategies, with the blocks turned on point, was the plan Elizabeth Noyd used for her quilt "Transitions." Her choice of darks and dark-mediums, and lights and light-mediums (with a few "just plain medium" values) is what makes this quilt reverberate.

Transitions by Elizabeth Noyd, 1990, Bellevue, Washington, 80" x 107". This quilt was designed for an antique sleigh bed and includes seventy-two different fabrics. Collection of Karl Mayer, Seattle, Washington.

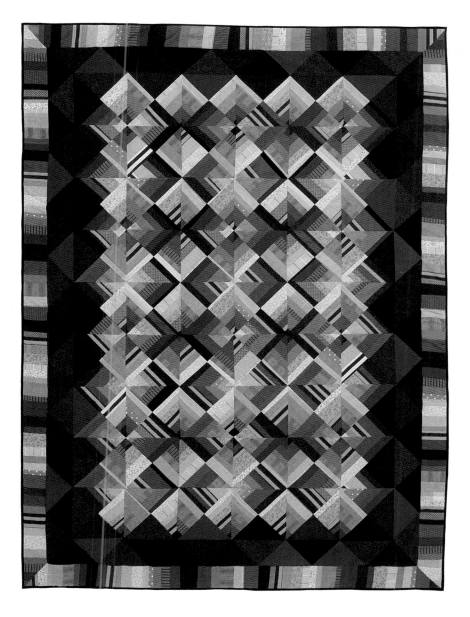

Senior Stripper by Ramona Crowell, 1987, Berkeley, California, 58" x 80". This was the quiltmaker's first full-size quilt.

One of your options is to combine patterns in the pieced surface, as Ramona Crowell did in her quilt "Senior Stripper." Not only did she alternate "A's to the Center" blocks with "Cs to the Center" blocks, she also alternated light and dark blocks within those four-block groupings.

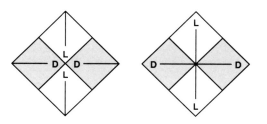

The last two rotations will yield diamonds of each chosen color family. If we repeat either of these rotations across a quilt surface, the resultant design will be a checkerboard of diamonds in the two color families.

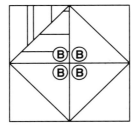

Blue Diamond by Marla J. Morris-Kennedy, 1991, Mequon, Wisconsin, 56" x 77". Multiple fabric borders effectively complement the block contents.

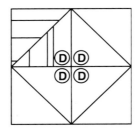

This is the design strategy used by Marla Morris-Kennedy in her quilt "Blue Diamond," shown at left. Notice the role that the lightest blue-striped fabric plays; it adds an extra shimmer to the surface and helps draw attention to the blue blocks.

Marla used the "Bs to the center" rotation; if she had used "Ds to the center," the stripe would not have been nearly as dramatic. (To see this effect, cover the first row of blocks on the left and the top row.)

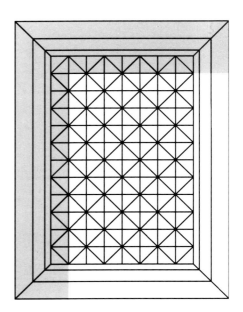

We could expand this idea of rotations beyond the single block, to rotating groups of blocks. Take the photographs of the "multiple-block checkerboards," (page 23), and cut them apart so you can rotate the individual light and dark "checkers."

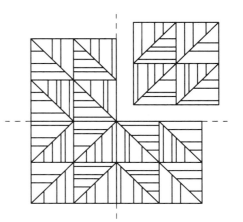

Try the rotations explained above, only this time, rotate the groupings of light or dark blocks, instead of only single blocks.

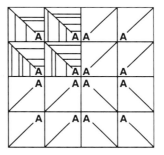

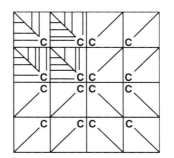

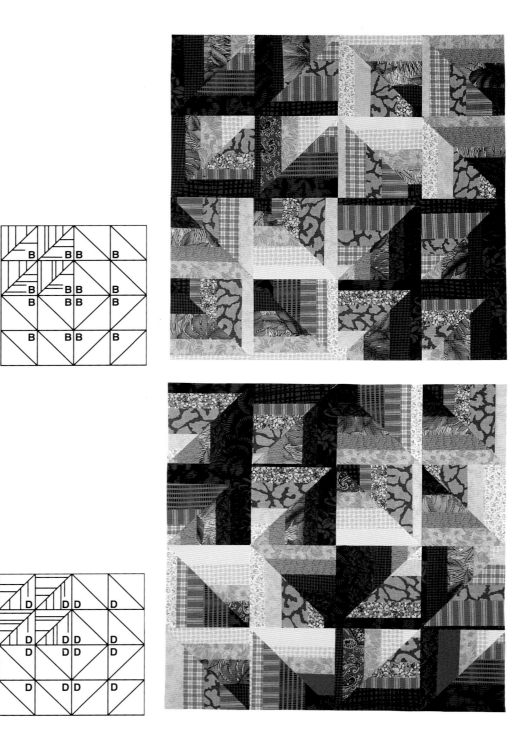

The units you rotate do not have to be a grouping of only light or dark blocks; all of the blocks do not have to be oriented the same way; and there are other kinds of rotations you might consider.

Wanda Hanson used the "A's to the center" rotation in her quilt "Sunset Strip," but she first created light and dark halves (corner to corner) of her sixteen-block units. The resultant pinwheel motif, one of her favorites, is especially dramatic because of the light-to-dark transition of values within each block.

Barbara J. Fowler chose two radiating designs as basic units in her rotation for "Banff to Jasper" (page 42). Note that the center four blocks have a different orientation than the blocks that surround them.

Sunset Strip by Wanda S. Hanson, 1991, Sandwich, Illinois, 44" x 44". The quiltmaker challenged herself to apply her favorite motif, the pinwheel, to the Strips That Sizzle blocks.

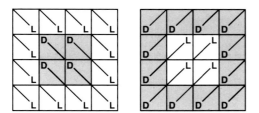

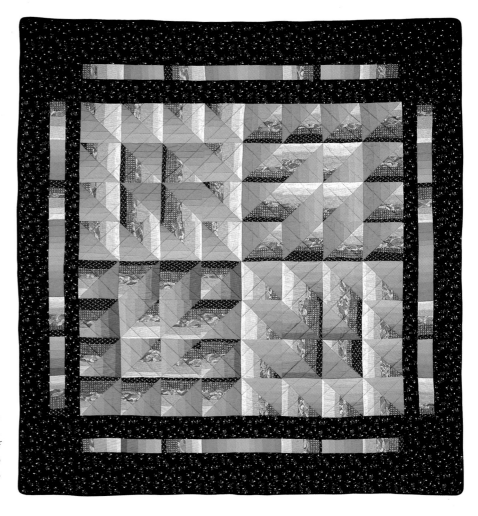

Banff to Jasper by Barbara J. Fowler, 1989, Newark, California, 74" x 80". This quilt was inspired by the colors of the Canadian Rockies during a 260-mile bicycle tour from Banff to Jasper in the summer of 1989.

This arrangement forms "phantom parallelograms," which seem to appear and disappear as you look at this piece.

Another design option is to take any given arrangement of blocks and try to highlight other aspects of the design by assigning colors or values differently. For example, Barbara Fowler's piece might be made up two more times, once to emphasize "circling birds" and another to highlight the parallelograms, as in the diagrams below.

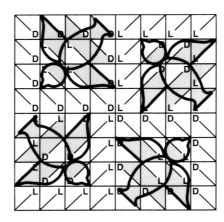
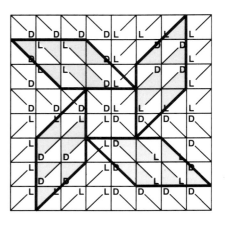

Multiple Rotations and Mirror Images

When we combine rotations and mirror images, another whole world of quilt design opens to us. In the following arrangements, the basic unit is not the single block but rather a combination of blocks.

For example, use two different pairs of mirror-image blocks atop each other as the basic unit.

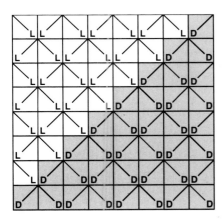
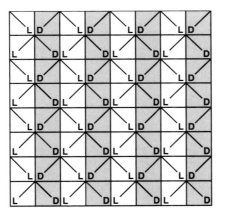
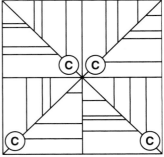

What do your blocks look like in the following light strategies, using this as the basic repeating unit?

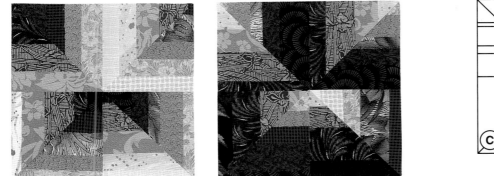

Now use the original block and one rotation in combination with its mirror image.

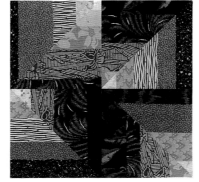
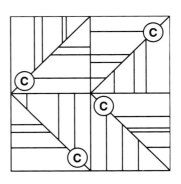

This block combination makes the color families form a zigzag pattern across the surface. What do your blocks look like in the following light strategies?

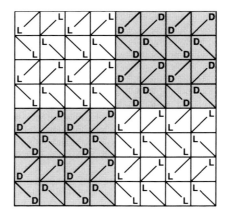 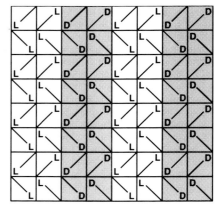

Still using the original block and one rotation, mirror image each of these vertically to form the following design as the basic building block.

One thing to keep in mind as you work with these designs and light strategies is that you are seeing only a tiny glimpse of what these arrangements would look like in a total quilt surface. For example, arrange your blocks in this design, using the following light strategy:

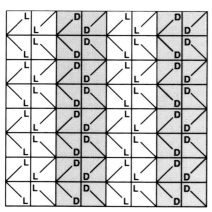 

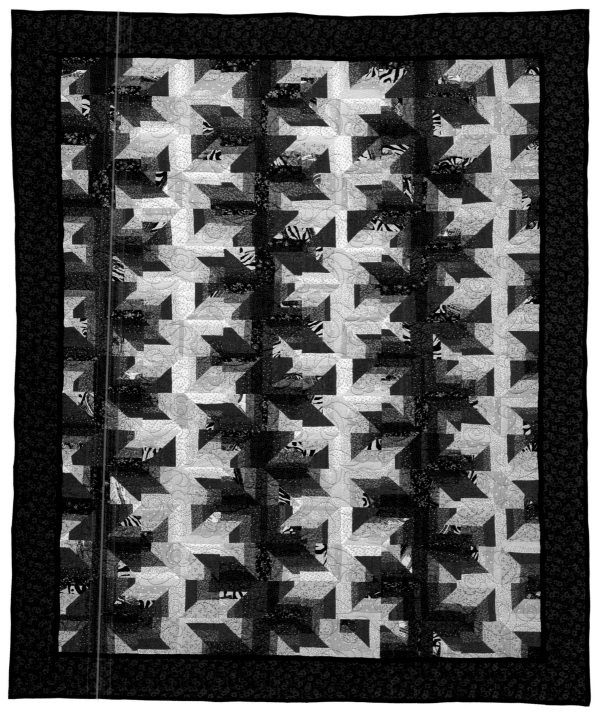

What you may see is floating, shadowed parallelograms as the dominant design; perhaps what you see doesn't make much visual sense. But look at Ola Bouknight's quilt "Stormy Sky" worked in this design and light strategy. The dominant visual impression is vertical dark and light columns.

Stormy Sky by Ola F. Bouknight, 1989, Bellingham, Washington, 75" x 92". One of a series of Strips That Sizzle quilts by this prolific quiltmaker; machine quilted by Patsi Hanseth, Mount Vernon, Washington.

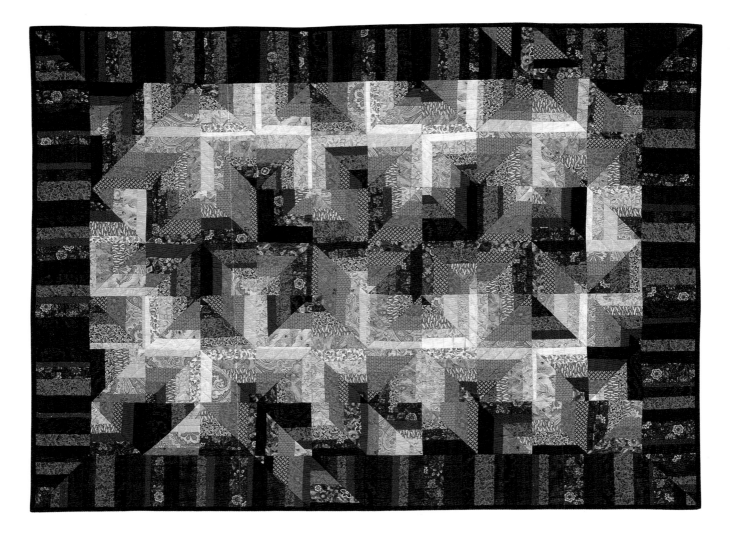

Ricochet by Sylvia S. Whitesides, 1991, Lafayette, Indiana, 62" x 48". Collection of Lafayette Family Physicians, Lafayette, Indiana.

Sylvia Whitesides used this pattern, turned sideways, as the focus of her quilt "Ricochet." However, she rotated some blocks in the outermost rows before the borders were added, which gives this pattern yet another feeling.

Now try some other light strategies with this design.

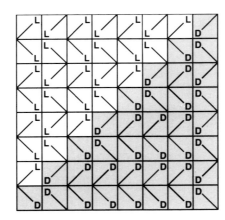

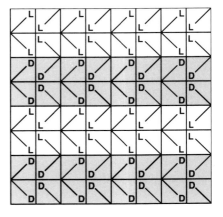

Surface Drawing with Bands of Color

Another world of design opens up when you connect color families to form pathways of bold color across the surface of the quilt. These drawing lines are actually an extension of the "Rotation by Row" motif discussed on page 29.

Blocks used as squares can produce diagonal bands of color; blocks "on point," or used as diamonds, result in horizontal or vertical bands, or a combination of the two.

Untitled quilt by Karen Hauser, 1991, Yakima, Washington, 55" x 55". Machine quilted in "fancy" machine stitching that required thirteen spools of thread, this quilt features forty different fabrics.

One obvious application of these "Strips That Sizzle color pathways" is to interpret Log Cabin patterns, with one color family representing the "dark" half and the other family representing the "light" half of the traditional Log Cabin block. Several sources of Log Cabin patterns are listed in the Bibliography on page 109. Use your blocks to interpret these patterns, paying attention to the depth your range of values adds to these traditional quilt layouts.

For example, Karen Hauser used the traditional Barn Raising arrangement of blocks in her untitled quilt. But, notice that she also took into account the light and dark values in her blocks to create a focus of light in the center of the quilt. This technique will be discussed at greater length in the section on "Color Strategies," beginning on page 52.

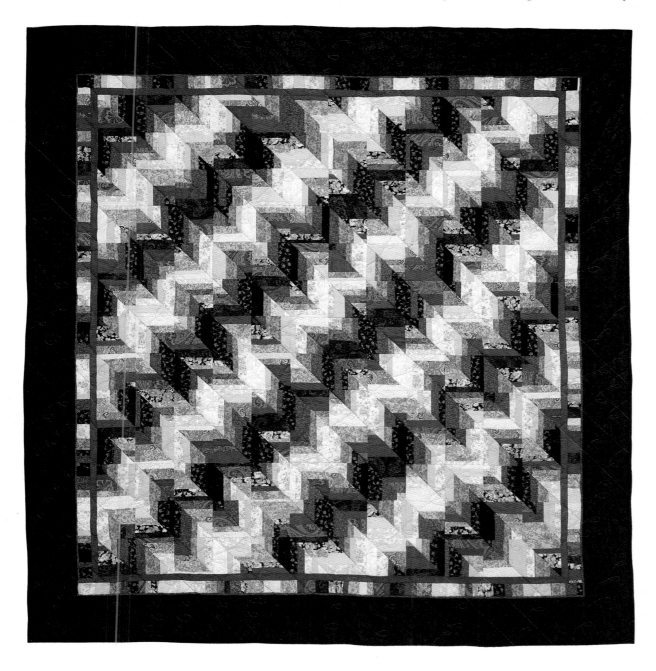

When working with the bold color pathways, do not lose sight of the placement of the light and dark values in the Strips That Sizzle blocks; these values allow you to add a glowing quality to this color pathway. For example, Caryn Jennings in her quilt "I Love the PNW Rain" aligned lights and darks along a diagonal line that is opposite the diagonal followed by the color paths. It gives the illusion that shafts of light (or perhaps trickles of water) are coming down a set of steps in this quilt.

I Love the PNW (Pacific Northwest) Rain by Caryn Jennings, 1991, Poulsbo, Washington, 79" x 83".

The Ocean Sun Dance by Gloria Marion, 1987, Del Mar, California, 79" x 40". The quiltmaker has taken to the extreme the effort to camouflage where the blocks stop and the border begins; the blocks appear to "escape" the border in places!

In her quilt "The Ocean Sun Dance," Gloria Marion created a meandering line with her color pathway, allowing it to escape the borders of the quilt in some areas. Notice that she also added a block, which is a square bisected by two diagonal lines; in this block, the "strips" feeling is reinterpreted, using a striped fabric.

Marty Hudlow also chose a meandering band of color as the design theme for her quilt "Road to Nowhere" (page 51, top). Notice that the band is a single diagonal row in some areas and a double row in others. The seemingly "individual" rust triangles in the upper left-hand corner are a good counterpoint to the wider double-row area of the design.

Road to Nowhere by Marty Hudlow, 1991, West Lafayette, Indiana, 39" x 45". This quilt "arranged itself" on the design wall once a "sparkle fabric" was added to the two basic color families.

Dawn Davis used a variation of the Barn Raising Log Cabin design in her "Noelia's Quilt," below. Notice the dappled light effect she achieved by alternating two rows of light blocks with two rows of dark blocks in this pattern.

Noelia's Quilt by Dawn Davis, 1991, Fresno, California, 101" x 80". Collection of Noelia Moreno-Carrera, an exchange student from Spain.

Color Strategies

In this chapter, we need to switch mental gears a bit. Up to this point, we have been focusing on specific block arrangements to achieve certain designs, or on specific, rather predictable ways of sprinkling light across certain areas of the quilt, such as creating horizontal stripes or checkerboards.

Now we need to look at the total picture—to look at the forest, not just the trees. In my first book, *Blockbuster Quilts* (That Patchwork Place, 1991), certain color strategies were discussed as a mechanism for "sprinkling light across the quilt surface," rather than agonizing about specific placement of specific fabric colors and values. Those same strategies can be applied to Strips That Sizzle quilts.

As you work with the various Strips That Sizzle layouts, you will soon come to a point where you will want to make more blocks to complete a given design idea, or to flesh out a small motif into a full-size quilt. At that point, you will probably have a pretty good idea of what you need. You may need to add more light fabrics to the original grouping of fabrics. Perhaps you need to add some dark mediums so that there is not such a sharp jump from your darkest value to your next darkest. You might want to eliminate a fabric that isn't working well in the arrangements you have tried so far.

One of your options when you get ready to make more blocks is to use more than just five or six values in any given color family. If you start with twelve values from dark to light, for example, in any given Strips That Sizzle block, you will have a definite "light," "medium," or "dark" feeling.

Let's say you are using twelve values of blue; number 1 is the lightest and number 12 is the darkest. If you are using a 6" acrylic template, you will be able to use only four or five of those twelve values in any given block. Each strip grouping below represents choices made from the twelve different values.

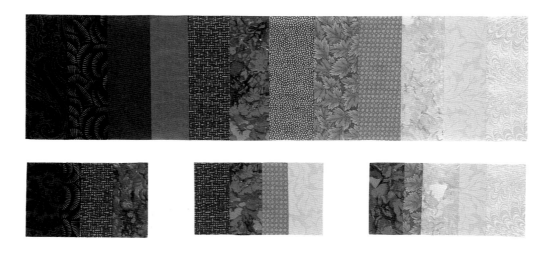

You can see how some strip groupings would look much lighter or darker than others.

If you used twelve values in the other family as well, you have the same options of creating some blocks that are very light, some that are a more medium value (even though the specific strips range from dark to light within the strip grouping), and some blocks that are very dark in both color families.

Carol Rothrock's quilt "Sherbet Skyline" is not technically a Strips That Sizzle quilt in that the strips that make up the blocks are all the same width and match at the diagonal seam. However, notice how Carol has used numerous values of the hand-dyed colors selected for this quilt; some blocks are half dark and half medium, some are dark on both sides, some light on both sides. You could explore this same effect with your Strips That Sizzle blocks if you used ten or twelve values in each color family rather than five or six values.

Sherbet Skyline by Carol R. Rothrock, 1991, Nordland, Washington, 33" x 37". This quilt is made with fabrics dyed by the quiltmaker.

Syncopation by Florence E. Peel, 1991, West Vancouver, British Columbia, Canada, 61" x 60". Certain of the darker values in the pink family become almost accent colors in this quilt.

Or, you may go from very light to very dark in one color family and have a more restricted range in the other. Florence Peel's quilt "Syncopation" is a good example of this combination. Though she uses very light through very dark families in her green family, she uses only very light through medium in the pink family. This arrangement sets up a delicate, gentle color area in the upper-left corner of the quilt, while a much more dramatic area appears in the lower-right corner because of the contrast of the very dark green values with the much lighter pinks in that area.

Angie Woolman used very light values in both color families to set up a "border within a border" in her quilt "Early Snow." Note that she used the same block arrangement as Caryn Jennings in "I Love the PNW Rain" (page 49) but has highlighted a certain area of it with very light values.

Obviously, one of your options is to use many values in one family and fewer values in the other. Another strategy would be to combine darker strips from one family with lighter strips from the other (as in Melon Patch, pages 27 and 88). If you then went back and created all the arrangements of the Strips That Sizzle blocks described earlier in this book, you can imagine how different the quilt surfaces would look from those you attained with your first set of Strips That Sizzle blocks.

It is important to remember that *all* of the light strategies discussed on pages 56–63 can be applied to *all* of the block arrangements described up to this point! The more you work with the Strips That Sizzle blocks, the better understanding you will have of the magic that movement of *value* across the quilt creates.

Early Snow by Angie Woolman, 1991, Albany, California, 45" x 54". Masterful use of light values create an "inner border" and add a special glow to this piece.

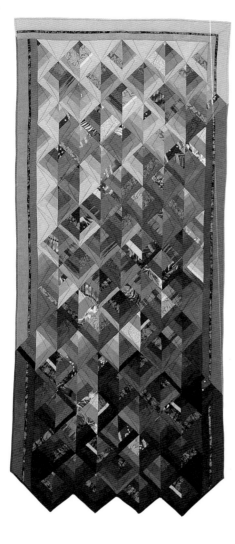

Horizontal Bands of Light

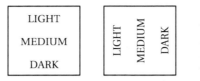

In this light strategy, pretend that there is a fluorescent tube across the top or along one side of your quilt; as your eye travels across the quilt, the light becomes weaker and weaker, and thus your values look darker.

This is the strategy used by Nancy Kies Miller in her quilt "Facets" (at left). Note that keeping the light values at the top does not mean that there are no medium or even dark values; it just means the predominant values in that area are light ones.

Spine of Light

In this strategy, it looks like a shaft of light is falling across the center of the quilt, either vertically or horizontally; as the eye travels to the edges of the quilt, the values darken. This shaft of light may also be placed off-center, for a less predictable effect.

Susan Wells Hall used this strategy in her quilt "The Hall Family Colors" (below). Even though the lightest values would be classified more properly as light-mediums or even mediums, the value movement is nevertheless from light in the center to dark at the top and bottom edges.

Facets by Nancy Kies Miller, 1990, San Carlos, California, 34" x 85". Purple fabrics were dyed by the quiltmaker; the innovative machine-quilting pattern helps carry out the theme of this quilt. Collection of Nick and Delyn Kies, Portland, Oregon.

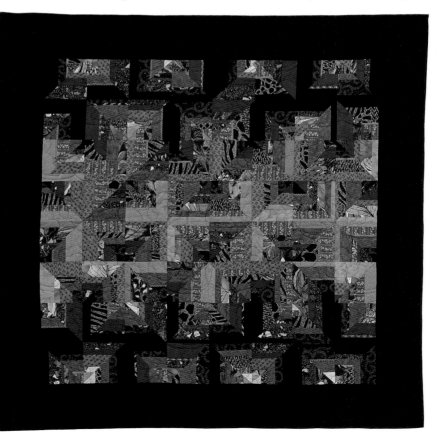

The Hall Family Colors by Susan Wells Hall, 1990, Mount Vernon, Washington, 51" x 51". A family friend, who noted that the quilt's colors reflected the colors commonly worn by the members of the Hall family, named this quilt. Machine quilted by Patsi Hanseth, Mount Vernon, Washington.

Centered Spotlight

A very common light strategy for quilts is to give the illusion that a spotlight is highlighting the center of the quilt. In this strategy, the lightest values are in the center of the quilt and are surrounded by an evenly distributed area of medium values, with the darkest values at the perimeter of the quilt.

Michelle Joanou used this light strategy in her dramatic quilt "Asilomar." Because of their sharp contrast with the background fabrics that extend to the edges of the quilt, her darks look even darker than they might have if she had used this strategy in a traditional way.

Asilomar by Michelle Joanou, 1991, La Canada, California, 52" x 52". The quiltmaker began this quilt in a workshop with Margaret J. Miller at the Empty Spools Seminar at Asilomar in Monterey, California.

Sizzler No. 1 by Phyllis A. Hughes, 1990, Wayne, Pennsylvania, 39" x 50". The concentration of light blocks in a pattern along block lines makes this quilt seem to glow.

This light strategy can be applied in a more specific way to block lines, as it is in Phyllis Hughes's quilt "Sizzler No. 1." Note that her lightest values are restricted to the area bound by the edges of the four diamonds in the center. Though this quilt does not go "down to the darks" as much as the previous quilt did, the general strategy is still light in the center to dark at the outer edges.

You can take any of these light strategies and reverse the positions of the lights and darks. Gloria Hunt did so in her quilt "A Touch of Gold." Note that this is virtually the same pattern as that used by Dawn Davis in "Noelia's Quilt" (page 51), with a slightly different treatment of the ends of the rays that emanate from the center of the quilt.

You can see how very different the same block arrangement can look in two different quilts, depending on the light strategy used. It may not be immediately obvious that the two quilts have a similar pattern.

A Touch of Gold by Gloria Hunt, 1991, Alameda, California, 78" x 78". The title comes from the choice of fabrics included in this quilt.

Spotlight from the Corner

The spotlight strategy outlined above can be used in other ways. The "spotlight" can hit the quilt off-center, or in the extreme, act like a floodlight shining near one corner of the quilt. One corner is illuminated brightly, but the light weakens quickly as you look at the rest of the quilt.

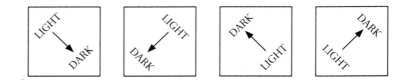

Beryl Sortino used this strategy masterfully with her quilt "Lavender's Green." Though most of this quilt is the same block arrangement used in Caryn Jennings's quilt (page 49) and Angie Woolman's quilt (page 55), there is one block that is rotated out of position, which adds even more drama to the brightly lit corner of this quilt.

Lavender's Green by Beryl S. Sortino, 1990, Absecon, New Jersey, 43" x 54". One block incorrectly positioned, according to the block arrangement in the balance of this quilt, adds visual interest.

Diagonal Shaft of Light

In this strategy, you have the illusion of a shaft of light, falling corner to corner across the quilt surface. The shaft of light fades into medium values and finally into darks in the opposite corners of the quilt.

Dale MacEwan used this shaft-of-light strategy in her quilt "Autumn Glow." You can almost see dappled sunlight coming through a grove of trees in autumn. Notice that the shaft of light does not have to be centered or on a corner-to-corner axis to be effective.

Autumn Glow by Dale MacEwan, 1991, Richmond, British Columbia, Canada, 42" x 42". This quilt was one of several that emerged as a result of several friends getting together to "play with" their Strips That Sizzle blocks.

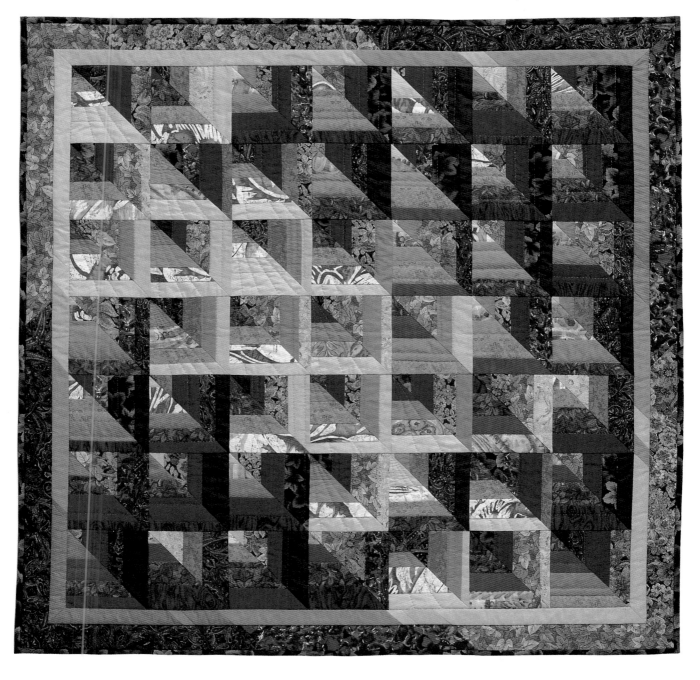

Magenta—A Little of What You Fancy Does You Good by Phyllis McFarland, 1990, Spokane, Washington, 90" x 90". An innovative integration of two very dissimilar pieced patterns: Strips That Sizzle and Drunkard's Path.

Phyllis McFarland used an unusual application of this light strategy in her haunting quilt, "Magenta—A Little of What You Fancy Does You Good." Note that she used this diagonal shaft-of-light strategy in the pieced blocks themselves, but the light does not extend to the corners of the quilt. Various points in the border seem to be illuminated by the source of light from the blocks, but not in a predictable way.

Another unusual application of this light strategy is Mary Lehmann's "Eye of the Storm." Note that her diagonal shaft of light is actually in what would technically be considered the border of the quilt; it is interrupted by the rectangular and significantly darker center. To dissect a quilt with the impact of this one seems almost a disservice; the power of this piece is surely greater than the sum of its parts.

Eye of the Storm by Mary L. Lehmann, 1991, Trumansburg, New York, 82" x 91". This quilt's center represents lightning; the value movement from top left to bottom right represents the storm moving in.

Columns by Margaret J. Miller, 1991, Woodinville, Washington, 68" x 67". This quilt combines two color strategies—one in the blocks and another in the pieced sashing strips.

Combining Color Strategies

You need not restrict yourself to only one color strategy in any given quilt. For example, in my quilt "Columns," one color strategy was used in the blocks (lighter pinks in the center columns, darker ones nearer the edges of the quilt), and another was used in the sashing strips. Six different values, from very light gray to black, were arranged in a checkerboard, step-wise fashion, in the sashing strips so that the values stay light at the top of the quilt and get darker as they approach the bottom. The "setting squares" were the same two light fabrics, arranged checkerboard fashion.

Sashing Strips and Strips That Sizzle

In many traditional quilts, the sashing strip gives your eyes a resting place so you can focus on the contents of the individual blocks, especially in sampler quilts. Often, in Strips That Sizzle quilts, you want to avoid interrupting the flow of light and pattern across the surface. However, adding sashing strips is a viable design option.

Using Plain Fabrics

If plain sashing strips separate every block in a traditional manner, you create the illusion of looking at a scene through a windowpane.

Hearthfires Endure by Margaret J. Miller, 1985, San Marcos, California, 59" x 59". This quilt features sashing strips in one direction only and incorporates blocks that are cut so the color families "jump the diagonal" to achieve the "folded ribbon" or "flame" effect.

Another option is to use sashing strips in one direction only, as in my quilt "Hearthfires Endure." In this quilt, the sashing strips are wider in the lower-right portion of the quilt and get progressively narrower as you approach the upper-left corner. Notice how the design changes as this narrowing of the sashing strips proceeds; the blocks can be visually related more easily, and the design takes on a completely different character. Instructions for a quilt like this one begin on page 97.

In my quilt "Boxes and Boxes," sashing strips graduate in size from the center of the quilt outward, but this time in both directions. Note that in any given quilt, just because sashing strips are used in some areas of the quilt, they do not have to be used throughout. This allows the flexibility of intensifying the design in some areas and "spreading it out" for a different visual impact in others.

When you change the width of the sashing strips, your blocks may no longer line up and form motifs as they did when no sashing strips were included. It is helpful to draw the blocks and sashing strips to scale

Boxes and Boxes by Margaret J. Miller, 1991, Woodinville, Washington, 73" x 92". This piece features sashing strips of varied widths, accented with contrasting setting squares.

on graph paper once you have played with the blocks on the design wall and have a general idea of what you want to do with them. I find that designing a Strips That Sizzle quilt with sashing strips is a process that proceeds simultaneously on graph paper and on the design wall. As the center portion of the quilt comes to life, I begin to play with various border ideas on graph paper.

Sashing strips may also be interrupted by a motif or a group of blocks, as they are in Lucinda Langjahr's quilt "Tilting at Windmills." Notice that in order to make the "north, south, east, and west" diamonds line up with the center four blocks, Lucinda added blocks of another size to compensate for the space remaining along the block edges after the sashing strips had been designed.

Using Pieced Fabrics

Another option is to use pieced fabrics in the sashing strips. A word of caution is in order, however. Do not allow the design of the sashing strips to overwhelm or distract from the visual impact of the blocks themselves.

Tilting at Windmills by Lucinda W. Langjahr, 1990, Bellevue, Washington, 62" x 72". This quilt is an unusual combination of pieced sashing strips and multiple block sizes, as well as an irregular shape.

I started the quilt "Columns" (page 64) with a set of blocks and the following criteria: 1) the blocks would be set on point, with the color families lined up to form columns; 2) they would be separated by pieced sashing strips; and 3) there would be two light strategies in the quilt, one in the sashing strips, another in the blocks themselves.

To create the border, only three templates were required.

Border Ideas for Strips That Sizzle

As you have seen, the drama of the Strips That Sizzle block comes from the interaction of values that flow across the surface of the quilt. The visual complexity of the quilt needs to be balanced or offset by a suitable border; single, solid bands of fabric would probably be too unlike the center.

This is not to say that it is always inappropriate to use solid-colored strips of fabric to "frame" a Strips That Sizzle quilt. Marla Morris-Kennedy's "Blue Diamond" (page 38) is a case in point; what makes this border successful is not only the change in color but the multiple strips of different widths and different values that complement the blocks it surrounds.

Just as you have found that the movement of light and motif camouflages where one block stops and its neighbor begins, you will find this design principle to be useful in border design. Try to camouflage where the Strips That Sizzle blocks stop and the border begins.

Not every Strips That Sizzle quilt needs a border; sometimes you may continue the fabric values or color families out to the edge of the quilt so that they become a backdrop for the central motif. They form a visual "breathing space" that tells the viewer that this quilt is complete, though no formal border is applied. You may create this visual rest area by substituting solid-colored triangles for some strip-pieced ones, or low-contrast Strips That Sizzle blocks, with the same color family on both sides of the block. An elegant example of the latter is Elizabeth Noyd's "Transitions" (page 36).

Carol Rothrock created this "visual breathing space" for her quilt "Sherbet Skyline" (page 53) with more of the strips used to make her original blocks. Notice how the blocks interact with this strip-pieced field differently on all sides of the quilt.

In her quilt "But, I Always Expected a Rose Garden," Doreen Rennschmid moved from lights at the top of the quilt to darks at the bottom. In addition, she moved from greens on the left to reds on the right by adding solid-colored fabrics as one triangle of her Strips That Sizzle blocks. Since these solid-colored fabrics are also included as strips in some of the strip-pieced triangles, the illusion is that parts of the strip-pieced

But, I Always Expected a Rose Garden by Doreen M. Rennschmid, 1990, Richmond, British Columbia, Canada, 84" x 68". A good example of the "lacy" effect you can achieve by using the same fabric in strips as well as solid triangles in a given quilt. Owned by Mary Sawatsky of Vancouver, British Columbia.

Rolling Thunder by Margaret J. Miller, 1985, San Marcos, California, 48" x 52". This quilt, which includes a significant number of solid fabric triangles for a Strips That Sizzle quilt, appeared in the Quilt National Exhibition in 1987.

blocks seem to "drop out" and become background. This gives areas of the quilt a "lacier" look. In this quilt, it creates the striking illusion of looking through a heavily planted rose garden.

The proportion of strip-pieced triangles or blocks to solid-colored ones can vary widely from quilt to quilt. In my quilt "Rolling Thunder," over a third of the blocks are either solid-colored fabrics, or half solid, half pieced. In this quilt, the strip-pieced blocks take on added significance because of the contrast of the orange triangles in the center and the design they create, and because the lightest blue values are used to consciously create a line design in the upper-left half of the quilt, which is then echoed by two other light blue fabrics.

In "Melon Patch" (pages 27 and 88), the addition of solid green triangles "stops the action" of the central motif in a very short distance. When the blocks of a quilt are placed "on point" as diamonds rather than squares, half-block triangles are required to create a square or rectangular quilt. In "Melon Patch," a black fabric was used for the outer triangles, which formed a kind of border, a visual "ending" for the quilt.

Such half-block triangles were only the jumping-off place for the border of Ramona Crowell's "Senior Stripper" (page 37). The solid-colored half-block triangles that form a straight edge around the blocks "on point" were repeated in an additional row all the way around the quilt; this was followed by straight bands of "leftover" strips. Notice that the contrast provided by the very dark solid-colored triangles makes the center of the quilt glow; the strip-pieced outer border provides the final touch for a well-integrated design.

Jean Perry used low-contrast, strip-pieced blocks in her quilt "Log Cabin Implosion." Even though the gray blocks are very low contrast, notice how Jean retained enough light-dark contrast so the parallelogram motifs extend out to the corners.

The center of "Log Cabin Implosion" is the same radiating design used in "Melon Patch" (pages 27 and 88); but notice that Jean used another motif, the parallelograms derived from "Rotation by Row" (page 29), to form an inner border.

Log Cabin Implosion by Jean M. Perry, 1990, Bayport, New York, 66" x 66". A striking example of incorporating three different effects possible with Strips That Sizzle blocks: a radiating design, a rotation design in high contrast, and a rotation design in low contrast.

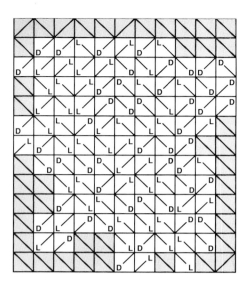

Another way of creating low-contrast areas is to continue blocks of only one color family out to the edges of the quilt. This was done in "Meanderings," which appears on page 92 and on the cover of this book. (See quilt plan at left.) The blocks of both color families (blue and red-orange) used in this quilt were sewn with "separators" between the values. (See "Design Diversions" chapter, page 79.) The fabric used in the separators on the blue side was also used as the solid-colored triangle in the blocks at the outer edges. This made the design formed by the orange triangles stand out in even greater relief. Notice that these border blocks not only appear in the outermost ring of blocks; they also appear *in an irregular pattern* within that outermost ring.

Another way to camouflage where the blocks stop and the border begins is to have the blocks "invade" the border area, as in Diana Smith's "Radiant Hearts" (below). This is yet another version of the design found in Gloria Hunt's "A Touch of Gold" (page 59) and Dawn Davis's "Noelia's Quilt" (page 51).

My quilt "Columns" (page 64) also features an "invaded" border. But in this case, the border is invaded by the sashing strips that surround each block. See Appendix B, page 106, for guidelines on how to make templates for borders, such as those used in "Radiant Hearts" and "Columns."

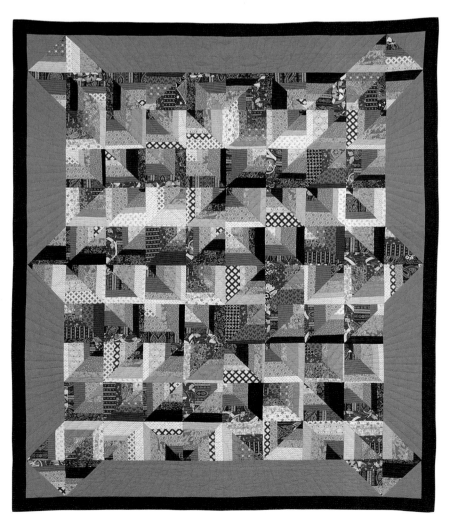

Radiant Hearts by Diana J. Smith, 1988, Anacortes, Washington, 52" x 63". This is the first full-size quilt made by this quiltmaker. Note the "phantom hearts" at the top and bottom of the quilt.

Since the Strips That Sizzle block is based on two triangles, the triangle motif is a natural choice as a jumping-off place for border design.

Diane Ross used the triangle as the key design element in the border plan for her quilt "Purple Mountain's Majesty." Notice the varied sizes and positions of the specific triangles used. The triangles in the border are larger than the triangles used in the center of the quilt, yet the complexity of the design that overflows from the center to parts of the border keep the entire quilt balanced.

Purple Mountain's Majesty by Diane Ross, 1990, Woodinville, Washington, 35" x 41". One factor that gives this art quilt such a contemporary look is the use of multisize triangles in the border.

Design Diversions

Firefall by Margaret J. Miller, 1982, San Marcos, California, 55" x 77". This quilt was an experiment in quilt shape as well as types of fabrics included. The black strips were cut from such fabrics as taffeta, poplin, cotton broadcloth, and polished cotton.

The following challenge categories are just a few of the many avenues you might explore in designing Strips That Sizzle quilts.

Single versus Multiple Color Families

Most of the quilts presented thus far were based on two color families. But, you can also challenge yourself by restricting yourself to one color family. Or, try using two families but sew them together in a different sequence; or cut strips from several different color families.

The quilt "Firefall" was started as a one-color-family quilt; the first blocks were made by sewing red, orange, raspberry, magenta, and other "generally red" strips together—just to see what would happen! Some grays, browns, and blacks were gradually added to the groupings of strips to introduce some darker values. Blocks were made according to the basic guidelines on pages 12–16; but instead of having two color families to keep track of, there was only one.

Another way to use two color families in a single quilt is exemplified by "Melon Patch" (page 88). Two color families, green and peach, were used, but instead of keeping the two families separated in their own strip groupings, *both* families were sewn into *every* grouping of strips. The strips were sewn together, going from dark to light in the strip grouping and following the original guidelines; but the darker values happened to be in the green family and the lighter ones in the peach family.

You may assign multiple color families to specific areas of the quilt, as Vicky Van Valkenberg did in her quilt "The Spirit of Carnaval." Vicky's quilt has an added dimension in that some of her color families "jump the diagonal." (See page 16.) In other words, in order to carry out the green area of the design, she cut some blocks with the green "against the table" and others with a different color against the table.

The Spirit of Carnaval by Vicky Van Valkenburg, 1991, Berkeley, California, 48" x 48". Though this quilt started as a way to "use up" leftover strips from other quilts, it soon took on a life of its own and required the cutting of extra strips from a dozen black fabrics to complete it.

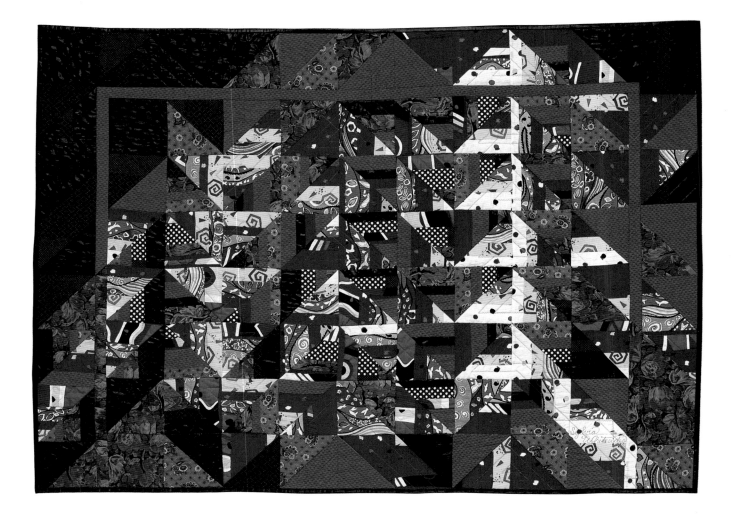

Depth Perception by Sylvia A. Whitesides, 1991, Lafayette, Indiana, 42" x 58". Colors for this quilt (red, yellow, green, and purple) could have been selected by placing a rectangle onto the color wheel. (See page 77.)

You may also use many color families in one quilt, as Sylvia Whitesides did in her exuberant quilt "Depth Perception."

Sylvia has not only used four color families (reds, yellows, greens, and purples), but one color family (reds) also appears on both sides of the block.

In some quilts, using the same fabric in every strip grouping can be distracting; the eye is too busy looking for places where strips of that single fabric come together at the diagonal seam to appreciate the movement of value in the rest of the quilt. Because of the intensity of the colors used in this piece, a single color on both sides of the square only adds to the gaiety.

Guidelines for Choosing Multiple Color Families

The first step to overcoming fear when choosing fabrics for a quilt is to realize that learning to use color is a lifelong endeavor. The more you try putting together fabrics of different color and value, the more you study color in other quilts, in nature, and in other types of art, the better you will use color in your own quilts.

Clear your mind of the "I can'ts" and play with the color wheel. Try to translate your experiments with the color wheel into real fabric. Consult some good books on color theory—perhaps very simple ones at first. (See the Bibliography on page 109.)

Start simply; begin with fabrics in monochromatic colors, all from the same color family. This is how the quilt "Firefall" (page 74) was started. Then, try to choose two or three fabrics in colors that are analogous, right next to each other on the color wheel.

When choosing two color families to use in the basic set of Strips That Sizzle blocks, the most dynamic colors are complementary colors, those opposite each other on the color wheel. These colors "bring out the best" in each other, completing each other as a harmonious pair.

When you are ready to use more than two color families in your quilting projects, try the system for selecting harmonious colors developed by Johannes Itten. Only a portion of his system is presented here; explore Itten's theories further and apply his principles to fabric after you get a feel for the basic color groupings presented here.

Trace the four templates (at right) onto paper or plastic and cut them out so they can be superimposed on the color wheel below.

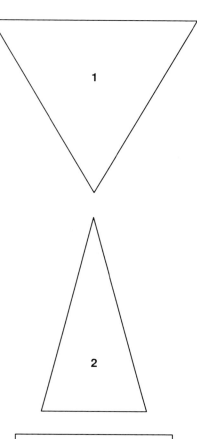

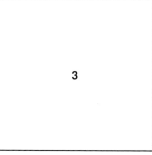

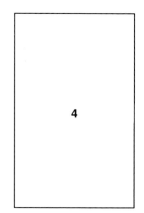

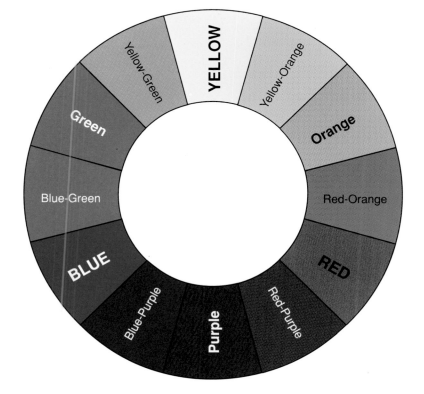

If you place either of the triangles onto the color wheel, the three color categories in which the points of the triangle fall are harmonious. Fabrics chosen from these categories would go well together in a quilt. The triangles can be rotated around the color wheel, thus choosing a number of harmonious triads. The equilateral triangle (template 1) can form four different color groupings, as seen in the diagram below.

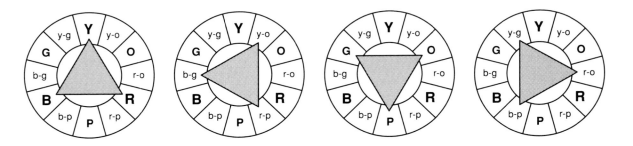

The isosceles triangle (template 2), however, can be rotated to select twelve different harmonious color triads. If you are very ambitious, do a quilt in each of those twelve groupings; after all, now you know how fast the Strips That Sizzle blocks can be made!

Another way to experiment is to involve a few of your adventurous quilting friends. Write the colors of each triad possible, using the isosceles triangle, on twelve slips of paper and place them in a basket. Have each friend draw a slip and then go home and make a quilt top using the colors she drew. Then, reassemble the group after a specified period of time to see and learn from each other's results!

For a less ambitious approach, select a triad of colors with which you are comfortable. Use fabrics that would fit into these three color families and arrange them from lightest to darkest in each of the three colors. Do this same exercise for three harmonious colors you have never used before in your quilts.

You can use the square and rectangle templates in the same manner to select harmonious pairs of complementary colors, or tetrads.

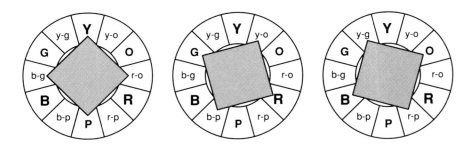

Notice that the square can be used to select three different four-color groupings in rotation around the color wheel, while the rectangle can be rotated to six different positions.

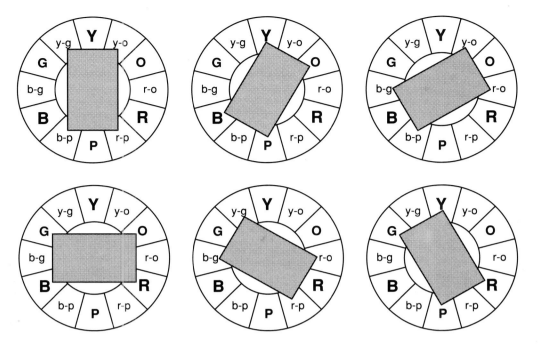

Using Separators

Up to this point, you have probably sewn your values together from darkest to lightest, one right next to the other. Another technique you might introduce into your group of blocks is adding a very narrow fabric between two or more values to create a space, or a separation. Using one or more such "separators" or "spacers" gives a very different character to the resultant Strips That Sizzle block.

The same principle applies here as with sashing strips; the more separators you use in any grouping of strips, the more the values become individual "stripes" within the block rather than "brush strokes of value" that interact with each other.

In order for separators to be effective, they must be different from the other strips in the grouping. Therefore, they might be

1. very light
2. very dark
3. a complementary color
4. a plaid fabric

Cut separator strips 1" or 1¼" wide at the most.

Sample strip groupings with separators

To begin experimenting with separators, consider using only one separator strip in a strip grouping of color family A in your original set of blocks; make some blocks from that grouping. Incorporate these new blocks into your basic set and make a number of block arrangements with them, to see how different the total group looks.

Then, either make more strip groupings using a single separator (still in color family A), or make strip groupings with multiple separators; all separators should be of the same fabric, cut the same width.

My quilt "Columns" (page 64) has separators in only the blue halves of the blocks. Furthermore, instead of using several values of blue fabric for the blue side of the block, I cut a single fabric into various strip widths, some of which were much wider than those given in the original guidelines. I used two different dark fabrics randomly as separators: a navy blue fabric with tiny white dots and a dark purple paisley print, which I also used as the darkest value on the pink side of the block.

Strip groupings were made with one, two, or three separators; notice that blocks with these separators were distributed across the quilt so that the blocks with the greatest number of separators were toward the bottom of the quilt; those with a single separator, which in some cases is so close to the point of the triangle that it looks like the triangle was cut from a single fabric, are nearer the top.

These separators bring areas of great contrast into the quilt, and a word of caution is in order: You *can* use too many separators in your quilt. For example, if all the blue triangles in "Columns" had three separators, the resultant surface would have been too busy, and the impact of the large blue print would have been diluted.

The quilt "Meanderings" (page 92) has separators on both sides of the block. On the blue side, the separators (cut 1¼" wide) are of a black-and-white, irregularly striped fabric. On the orange side, a much narrower, bright blue separator unites the two color families across the quilt.

Using Multiple Block Sizes

The blocks in your basic set were made 6" or 6½" square because of the convenience of the acrylic cutting guides that are currently available, and because one can see the entire quilt easier with smaller blocks. However, you may use blocks in a variety of sizes in a single quilt, or you may use a block very much larger or very much smaller than 6".

If you do use tiny blocks, you will probably want to cut your strips in only a narrow range of widths to get the necessary visual variety from block to block. Keep in mind that the smaller the Strips That Sizzle block, the "stiffer" the quilt surface becomes because of the numerous seam allowances in a small area.

If you want to use separators in your blocks, use a larger block size to accommodate four or five values in any strip grouping.

In general, cut your blocks 1" larger than you want your finished blocks to be. For 6" finished blocks, cut 7" blocks from your strip groupings. The diagonal seam takes up some seam allowance, and the blocks are sewn to each other, using a ¼"-wide seam allowance. To ensure accurate piecing and a flat quilt top, trim each block to a uniform size after the diagonal seam has been sewn or after you have "played" with the blocks on the design wall and have decided on a final quilt plan.

The photo (at left) shows a number of Strips That Sizzle blocks of various sizes.

The most efficient use of the 22"-long strip groupings is a 6" or 6½" block; you can cut three sets of Strips That Sizzle blocks from each strip grouping.

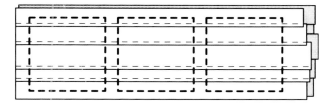

(If you are careful, you might be able to cut three blocks, each 7" x 7", from each strip grouping.)

Once your blocks get larger than 7", however, you will be able to cut only two blocks per strip grouping. When cutting squares larger than 7" from the strip groupings, you will have some leftover strips that you might be able to incorporate into your border, as in Ramona Crowell's "Senior Stripper" (page 37), Sylvia Whitesides's "Ricochet" (page 46), or Barbara Fowler's "Banff to Jasper" (page 42).

Combining Motifs and Transforming Patterns

Once you are at ease with a few of the block configurations and light strategies of your Strips That Sizzle blocks, and you have gone on to make more blocks to flesh out the basic grouping of thirty blocks with which you started, you will be ready to "cut loose" and see where the blocks lead you, rather than trying to follow any given pattern arrangement .

Challenge yourself to start with one pattern in the quilt and transform it as it travels across the quilt surface. This idea was the inspiration for the quilt "Meanderings" (page 92). This quilt has a number of motifs (rotations, solid bands of color, "weaving" of solid bands) in various parts of the quilt. One of the design goals of this quilt was to have all four corners and all four edges of the quilt different from each other.

Another good example of this "letting go" and letting the quilt tell the quiltmaker what to do next, is Diane Ross's "Purple Mountain's Majesty" (page 73). Diane not only used blocks that were cut so the color families "jumped the diagonal" (page 16), but she also introduced triangles of various sizes in the border to make her Strips That Sizzle blocks sing a new song.

Quilt Projects

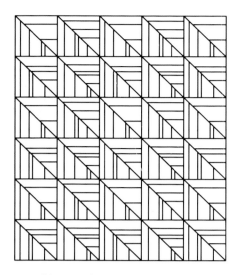

Possible quilt layout

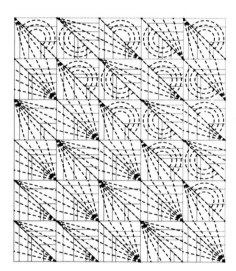

The quilts in this chapter have appeared earlier in this book and were selected to give you experience making Strips That Sizzle quilts with 1) all strip-pieced blocks, 2) blocks combining strip-pieced and solid-colored triangles, 3) blocks with separators, and 4) sashing strips.

Strips That Sizzle quilts are unique in that specific colors of certain solid-colored or printed fabrics cannot be prescribed for specific shapes or areas of the quilt. Fabric requirements are listed in terms of value ranges instead of color and print descriptions. It is important to spend some time arranging your basic set of thirty blocks in a number of the configurations presented earlier in this book before you begin any of the preplanned projects. Your understanding of your fabrics and of the values you have chosen (and the other values you may wish to add) will affect the visual outcome of any of the following projects.

Likewise, specific yardages cannot be listed as accurately as they can for traditional quilt projects. Fabric requirements are stated as specifically as possible, but there will probably be a few strips left over that you can incorporate into the quilt backing. Leave yourself open to adding a fabric or two from your general supply of fabrics, or perhaps dropping out one of the fabrics cut for any given project, for the maximum visual impact from your strips and blocks.

General Guidelines for Piecing

A few general piecing hints are in order before starting the specific project directions. First, when stitching the diagonal seam to join the triangles, stitch slowly; you are dealing with bias edges and many seam allowances. Press the diagonal seam allowance toward the same color family in every block; this will help distribute bulk when the blocks are joined together. Some people like to trim off the little triangles that peek out beyond the finished block after the diagonal seam is sewn, but it is not necessary.

Ideally, your quilt will be arranged in the desired configuration on a design wall or on a flat surface. To assemble the quilt, remove blocks by row, stacking the blocks in order from the bottom of the quilt to the top, or from left to right. I usually insert a straight pin at the border edge of the block at the end of the row; then, when all the blocks are sewn together, it is easy to place the row back on the wall in the right direction (not upside down!).

Press seam allowances of diagonal block seams toward one color; as blocks are sewn together, you may need to press some of these seams toward the other color in order to reduce bulk at the corners of blocks.

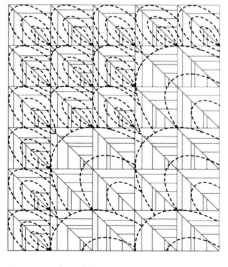

Suggested quilting patterns

Press seam allowances between joined blocks in one direction in the first row of blocks and in the opposite direction in the next row as indicated by the arrows in the diagram below. Repeat across the entire quilt. This will make matching the seams easier when joining completed rows and will distribute evenly the bulk of the seam allowances.

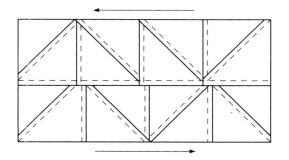

General Notes on Finishing

Other materials not specifically listed below are batting, backing, and binding fabrics. Use any strips or blocks that may be left after the quilt top is completed to make a unique backing for your Strips That Sizzle quilt.

Sandwich the completed quilt top with batting and backing and quilt as desired. Quilting designs that have curves or undulating, wavy lines and designs that flow from one block to another or extend across many blocks, regardless of block boundaries, are more effective than quilting "in the ditch" at seam lines.

Use your favorite binding technique, or consult Mimi Dietrich's book *Happy Endings* (published by That Patchwork Place) to finish the quilt edges.

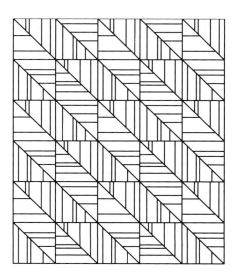

Possible quilt layout

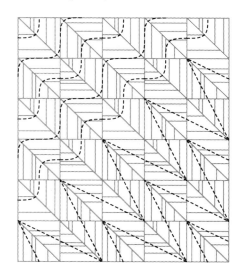

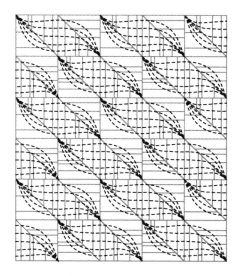

Suggested quilting patterns

*Fractured Pansies by Wanda S. Hanson,
1991, Sandwich, Illinois, 54" x 42". The
quiltmaker combined newly available
yellows and golds with purples she had
collected to create this dazzling design.*

Fractured Pansies

This quilt was made by Wanda Hanson of Sandwich, Illinois; she has generously allowed me to share the instructions for making it.

Dimensions: 53" x 38"
Finished Block Size: 5"
Number of Blocks Required: 30 light and 30 dark

Materials: 44"-wide fabric
½ yd. each of the following for blocks:
   8 values of color family A (purple)
   8 values of color family B (gold)
1 yd. for border triangles (dark purple)
Batting, backing, binding, and thread to finish

Blocks

1. Fold each fabric in color families A and B in half, selvage to selvage, and cut along fold. Layer fabrics in stacks of 3 or 4 values (6 or 8 fabric layers) and make 1 crosscut of each in the following widths: 2½"; 2¼"; 2"; 1¾"; and 1½". (You should have 2 strips of each of these widths from each of the fabrics in the stack.)
2. Working with one color family at a time, arrange the strips from dark to light on the table or other work surface.
3. Assemble 10 strip groupings in each color family, following the guidelines on pages 13–15 and making sure that you don't always start with the same dark fabric or end with the same light.
4. Cut the paired strip groupings into 6" squares and make 60 blocks (30 dark and 30 light), following the general guidelines on pages 15–16.

Border and Corner Triangles

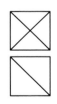

1. From the dark purple for border triangles, cut 5 squares, each 13½" x 13½"; cut twice diagonally to yield 20 border triangles.

2. Cut 2 squares, each 9½" x 9½"; cut once diagonally to yield 4 corner triangles.

Quilt Construction

1. Arrange your Strips That Sizzle blocks and corner and border triangles on your design wall, following the diagram at right.

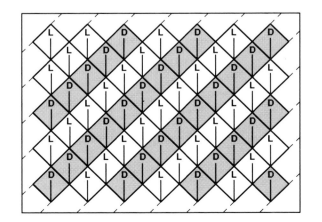

2. Sew blocks together in diagonal rows, adding border triangles as shown.

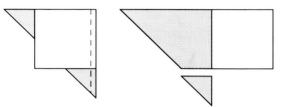

Side: Align square corners of block and triangle; stitch. Trim after pressing.

Press seams so they lie in opposite directions, row to row.

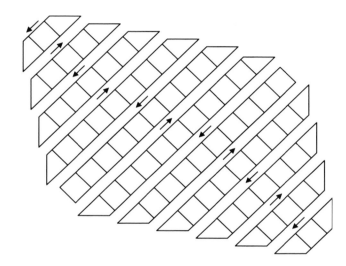

3. Sew completed rows together.
4. Center the long edge of each corner triangle over a corner of the quilt. Stitch; press.

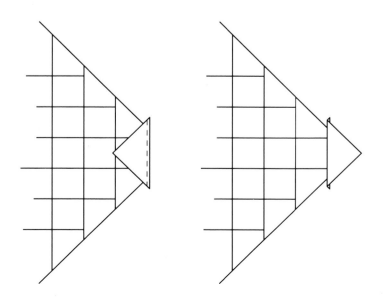

5. To square off quilt, line up acrylic ruler so the 1½" line is along the finished block corners on one edge and trim excess with rotary cutter. Repeat on remaining edges of quilt.

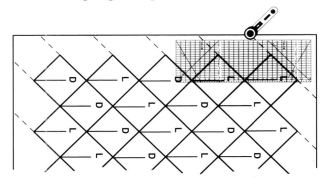

6. Layer quilt top with batting and backing; baste. Quilt as desired and bind the edges.

Melon Patch by Margaret J. Miller,
1982, San Marcos, California, 55" x 55".
This quilt was part of the 1985 Quilt
National Exhibition in Athens, Ohio.

Melon Patch

In this quilt you will use your two color families differently than in previously described Strips That Sizzle quilts: in Melon Patch, you will sew both color families into each strip grouping.

Dimensions: 55" x 55"
Finished Block Size: 7½"
Number of Blocks Required:
   13 dark blocks with both halves strip pieced
   16 light blocks with both halves strip pieced
   6 dark blocks with one-half strip pieced and one-half a solid-colored triangle
   6 light blocks with one-half strip pieced and one-half a solid-colored triangle

Materials: 44"-wide fabric
½ yd. each of the following for blocks:
   6 dark to medium values of color family A (green)
   6 medium to light values of color family B (peach)
¾ yd. solid-colored fabric of color family A (green) for the solid half-blocks
⅝ yd. black for border and corner triangles
Batting, backing, binding, and thread to finish

Blocks

1. Set aside fabric for solid halves of the pieced/solid blocks. Fold each of the fabrics for the blocks in color families A and B in half, selvage to selvage, and cut along the fold. Layer fabrics in stacks of 3 or 4 values (6 or 8 fabric layers) and make 1 crosscut of each in the following widths: 2½"; 2¼"; 2"; 1¾"; and 1½".
2. Working with *both color families at the same time*, arrange all strips from dark to light on your work surface. The dark values should be in one color family and the lighter ones in the other color family.
3. Assemble 18 strip groupings, making them wide enough to cut 8½" squares from them. Follow the guidelines on pages 13–15, making sure that you don't always start with the same dark or end with the same light.
4. Cut the paired strip groupings into 8½" squares and make 32 blocks (16 darks and 16 lights), following the general guidelines on pages 15–16. For this quilt, you can ignore the "same color against the table" rule. You should have at least 2 strip groupings left after making the required number of blocks.
5. To make the strip-pieced/solid-triangle fabric blocks, use the solid-colored fabric of color family A set aside earlier and the leftover strip groupings from step 4, above.

   Fold the solid-colored fabric in half, selvage to selvage, and cut along the fold. From the double layer of fabric, cut 2 strips, each 9" wide.

   Place the wrong side of a leftover strip grouping on the table with the "darks in your lap" and place a solid-colored strip on top, right sides together. Cut one 8½" square. Repeat this layering process 2 times, using a different strip grouping each time and cutting one 8½" square each time. You should have a total of three 8½" squares, cut with the strip groupings on the bottom.

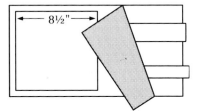

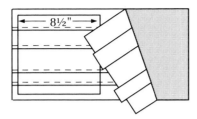

Place the wrong side of a solid-colored strip on the table and place a leftover strip grouping on top, right sides together. Cut one 8½" square. Repeat this layering process 2 more times, using a different strip grouping each time and cutting one 8½" square each time. You should have a total of three 8½" squares, cut with the strip groupings on the top.

6. Using the 6 sets of squares just cut, make 12 Strips That Sizzle blocks, following the general guidelines on pages 15–16.

Border and Corner Triangles

1. From the black fabric, cut 4 squares, each 14½" x 14½"; cut twice diagonally to yield 16 border triangles.

2. Cut 2 squares, each 10" x 10"; cut once diagonally to yield 4 corner triangles.

Quilt Construction

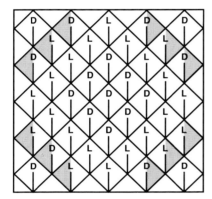

1. Arrange the Strips That Sizzle blocks and the border and corner triangles on your design wall, following the diagram at left.
2. Sew the blocks and triangles together in diagonal rows, adding border triangles as shown.

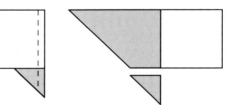

Side: Align square corners of block and triangle; stitch.
Trim after pressing.

Press seams so they lie in opposite directions, row to row.

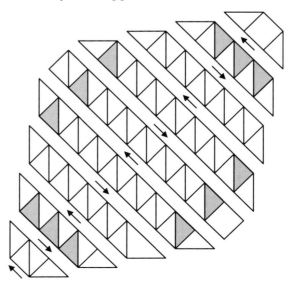

3. Sew completed rows together.
4. Center the long edge of each corner triangle over a corner of the quilt. Stitch; press.

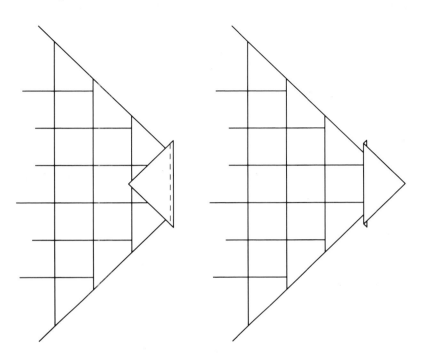

5. Square up the outer edges of the completed quilt top. Trim any excess from the outside edges of the corner and border triangles, leaving a ¼"-wide seam allowance beyond the corners of the finished Strips That Sizzle blocks as shown.

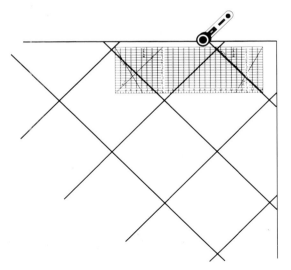

6. Layer quilt top with batting and backing; baste. Quilt as desired and bind the edges.

Meanderings by Margaret J. Miller, 1991, Woodinville, Washington, 72" x 85". This quilt weaves together solid bands of color formed by the Strips That Sizzle blocks.

Meanderings

I made this quilt for the challenge of transposing the design as it moves across the quilt surface. I also wanted to create a quilt with no two edges or corners identical.

Dimensions: 72" x 85"
Finished block Size: 6½"
Number of Blocks Required:
  50 dark blocks with both halves strip pieced
  51 light blocks with both halves strip pieced
  21 dark blocks with one-half strip pieced and one-half a solid-colored triangle
  21 light blocks with one-half strip pieced and one-half a solid-colored triangle

Materials: 44"-wide fabric
½ yd. each of 8 dark to light values of color family A (orange)
¾ yd. each of 8 dark to light values of color family B (blue)
2 yds. print in color family B for solid triangles and separators
¼ yd. color family A for separators
Batting, backing, binding, and thread to finish

Blocks

1. Fold each fabric in color families A and B in half, selvage to selvage, and cut along fold. Layer fabrics in stacks of 3 or 4 values (6 or 8 fabric layers) and make 2 crosscuts of each in the following widths: 2½"; 2¼"; 2"; and 1¾". (You should have 4 strips in each of these widths from each of the fabrics in the stack.)
2. Fold separator fabric for color family A in half, selvage to selvage, and cut along fold. Cut as many 1"-wide strips as you can from the ¼ yard of fabric. (You should have at least 16 strips, each 1" x 22".)
3. Fold the printed fabric in color family B in half, selvage to selvage, and then in half crosswise so you have 4 layers of fabric. Cut along the crosswise fold and then along the lengthwise fold (parallel to the selvages). Make 2 crosscuts, each 8" wide. You should have 8 strips of this width.

Cut the remaining fabric layers into as many 1½"-wide strips as possible to use as separators with the strips of color family B.
4. Working with one color family at a time, arrange the strips from dark to light on the table or other work surface.

5. Make all strip groupings described below wide enough so you can cut 7½" squares from them.

   a. Assemble 17 strip groupings in color family A. Make 3 of these groupings, following the guidelines on pages 13–15. Add 1, 2, or 3 of the narrow separators to each of the other 14 groupings.

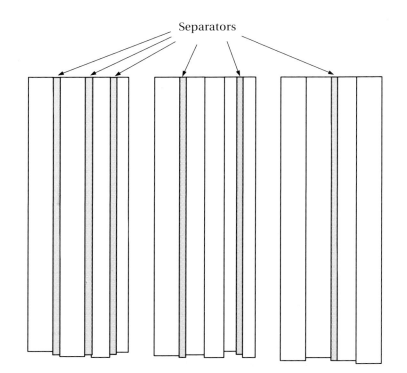

Sew single and multiple separators between different pairs of strips in each grouping.

   b. Assemble 24 strip groupings in color family B. Make 13 of these groupings in which you add, at random, 1 or 2 separators to the grouping. Make 7 strip groupings in which you add a separator between each pair of strips. Set these aside to use with the printed fabric (family B). Make 4 strip groupings without separators, following the guidelines on pages 13–15 and making sure that you don't always start with the same dark fabric or end with the same light.

6. Using strip groupings, make 102 strip-pieced blocks (51 dark and 51 light). Follow the general guidelines on pages 15–16, making sure that the same color family is always against the table when you layer the groupings for cutting.

7. Place 1 of the 7 strip-pieced groupings from color family B set aside in step 5, above, on the table, right side up. Place a strip of printed fabric from step 3, page 93, on top, right sides together. Cut 42 squares, each 7½" x 7½", and assemble, following the general guidelines on pages 15–16. You should have 21 dark blocks and 21 light blocks.

Quilt Construction

1. Arrange the Strips That Sizzle blocks on your design wall, following the quilt diagram below.

   Note: Blocks with only a diagonal line (no "L" or "D" in the block) represent solid/strip-pieced blocks.

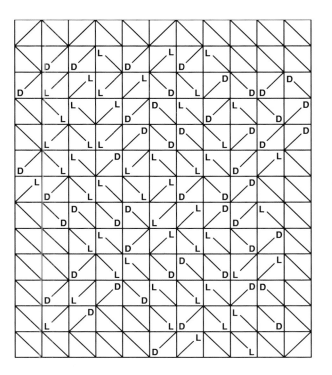

2. Sew blocks together in horizontal rows, pressing seams so they lie in opposite directions, row to row. Sew completed rows together.
3. Layer quilt top with batting and backing; baste. Quilt as desired and bind the edges.

*Hearthfires Endure by Margaret J. Miller,
1985, San Marcos, California, 59" x 59".
This quilt features sashing strips in one
direction only and incorporates blocks
that are cut so the color families "jump
the diagonal" to achieve the "folded
ribbon" or "flame" effect.*

Hearthfires Endure

I made this quilt in 1985 as an experiment in varying the width of sashing strips, as well as in using the triangle as the basic design unit rather than the square.

Dimensions: 59" x 59"
Finished Block Size: 5"
Number of Blocks Required:
   27 blocks with strip piecing on both halves of the block
   35 blocks with one-half strip pieced and one-half a solid-colored triangle

Materials: 44"-wide fabric
½ yd. each of 6 values of color family A (orange)
½ yd. each of 6 values of color family B (blue)
3½ yds. dark solid (blue) for sashing strips and outer edges
Batting, backing, binding, and thread to finish

Blocks

1. Fold each fabric in color families A and B in half, selvage to selvage, and cut along fold.
2. Set aside 1 layer of each fabric. Place the remaining layers in stacks of 6 fabrics. From each stack, cut one 6"-wide strip.
3. From the remaining layer of each fabric, cut 1 strip of each in the following widths: 2½"; 2¼"; 2"; 1¾"; and 1½".
4. Working with one color family at a time, arrange the strips from dark to light on the table.
5. Assemble 15 strip groupings in color family A (orange) and 9 groupings in color family B (blue). Follow the guidelines on pages 13–15, making sure that you don't always start with the same dark or end with the same light.
6. Cut 6" blocks, following the guidelines on page 98, but do not sew the diagonal seam. Arrange the paired triangles on the design wall in the configuration shown below, leaving space for sashing strips between diagonal rows. After all the border shapes are cut and placed on the design wall, you may want to rearrange the triangles to develop your own variation of this quilt.

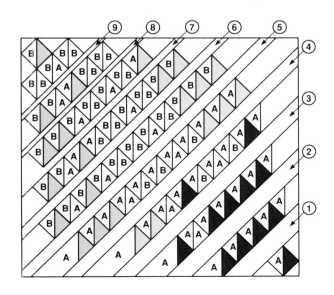

A = strip-pieced triangles, color family A (orange)

B = strip-pieced triangles, color family B (blue)

▶ = solid fabric triangles, color family A (orange)

▷ = solid fabric triangles, color family B (blue)

Numbers refer to sashing strips.
See page 99 for cutting directions.

Block 1   Use: 2 solid blue strips;
6 blue strip groupings.

               Stack: solid blue strip on table;
blue strip grouping on top.

               Cut: 6 squares to yield 12 paired triangles (blocks).

Note: Remember to place a different blue strip grouping on top of the solid blue strip on the table every time you cut a new square. Keep this in mind when cutting all paired triangles for the "blocks" that follow.

Block 2   Use: 2 blue strip groupings;
6 blue strip groupings from Block 1.

               Stack: 2 different blue strip groupings, right sides
together.

               Cut: 6 squares to yield 12 paired triangles (blocks).
You will use only 11 pairs.

Block 3   Use: 2 orange strip groupings;
6 blue strip groupings from Block 2.

               Stack: orange strip grouping on table;
blue strip grouping on top.

               Cut: 5 squares to yield 10 paired triangles (blocks).
You will use only 9 pairs.

Block 4   Use: 2 solid blue strips;
5 orange strip groupings.

               Stack: solid blue strip on table;
orange strip grouping on top.

               Cut: 5 squares to yield 10 paired triangles (blocks).
You will use only 9 pairs.

Block 5   Use: 1 blue strip grouping;
3 orange strip groupings from Block 4.

               Stack: blue strip grouping on table;
orange strip grouping on top.

               Cut: 3 squares to yield 6 paired triangles (blocks).

Block 6   Use: 1 orange strip grouping;
3 orange strip groupings from Block 5.

               Stack: 2 different orange strip groupings, right sides
together.

               Cut: 3 squares to yield 6 paired triangles (blocks).

Block 7   Use: 2 solid orange strips;
3 orange strip groupings from Block 6.

               Stack: solid orange strip on table;
orange strip grouping on top.

               Cut: 6 squares to yield 10 paired triangles (blocks).

In addition to the paired triangle "blocks" you have just cut, you will need the following single triangles:

Place 1 solid blue strip on table, right side up. Cut 1 square; cut once diagonally to yield 2 triangles.

Place 1 orange strip grouping on table, right side up. Cut 2 squares; cut once diagonally to yield 4 triangles.

Place 1 dark orange strip on table, right side up. Cut 1 square; cut once diagonally to yield 2 triangles.

Sashing

1. Cut the following strips from the dark solid (blue).
   Strip 1: 5" x 25½"
   Strip 2: 5½" x 42½"
   Strip 3: 4" x 59½"
   Strip 4: 3½" x 75½"
   Strip 5: 3" x 80½"
   Strip 6: 2½" x 66½"
   Strip 7: 2" x 52½"
   Strip 8: 1½" x 39½"
   Strip 9: 1½" x 27½"
2. Place sashing strips on your design wall, following the diagram on page 97. Now is the time to play with the block arrangement to develop your personal variation of this quilt.

Border Units

1. To construct the border units shown in the quilt diagram on page 97, first cut the following bias strips from the dark solid (blue):
   Strip B2: 5½" x 11"
   Strip C2: 5½" x 14"
   Strip D2: 5½" x 17½"
   Strip E2: 5½" x 17"
   Strips F1 and F2: each 5½" x 11½"
   Strips G1 and G2: each 5½" x 9½"
   Strips H1 and H2: each 5½" x 8"
   Strips J1 and J2: each 5½" x 7" (There are no I strips.)
2. Cut the following strips from orange strip groupings:
   Strip B1: 5½" x 10½"
   Strip C1: 5½" x 14½"
   Strip D1: 5½" x 18"
   Strip E1: 5½" x 16"

3. Draw diagonal lines on the right side of the blue strips and the orange strips (strip grouping) as shown. Using a rotary cutter and an acrylic ruler, cut on the diagonal lines and discard the small triangles.

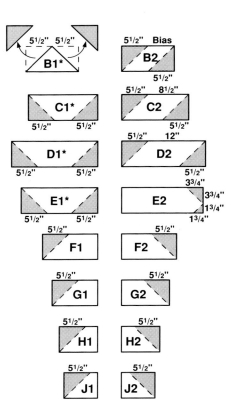

*Cut from orange strip groupings.

Place each shape in position on the design wall as you cut it, referring to the quilt diagram below.

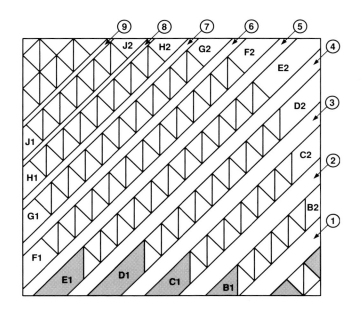

Border and Corner Triangles

1. With a solid orange strip on the table and orange strip grouping on top, right sides together, cut one 6" square. Cut in half as shown. Position 1 pair of the resulting triangles on the design wall in the space remaining at the bottom edge in the lower-right corner.

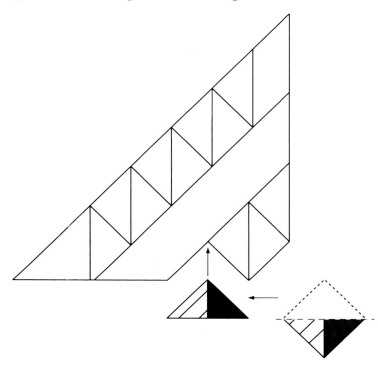

2. From solid blue fabric, cut one 10½" square. Cut twice diagonally to yield 4 triangles. Position on design wall in the space remaining on adjacent sides of upper-left corner.

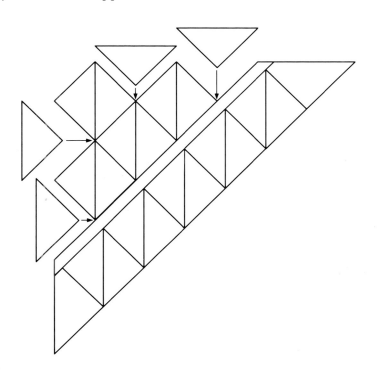

3. From solid blue fabric, cut one 7½" square. Cut once diagonally to yield 2 corner triangles. Place in position at upper-left and lower-right corners on design wall.

Quilt Construction

1. Working in diagonal rows, sew triangles into blocks, using ¼"-wide seam allowances.
2. Sew blocks and border units into diagonal rows. Press seams so they lie in opposite directions, row to row.
3. Sew completed rows together with sashing strips centered between them, making sure that the block seams line up before stitching.

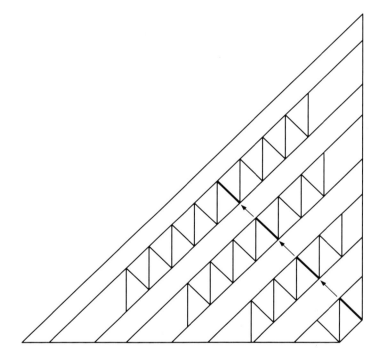

4. Center the corner triangles over the upper-left and lower-right corner blocks and stitch.
5. True up edges of quilt, using a rotary cutter and an acrylic ruler.
6. Layer quilt top with batting and backing; baste. Quilt as desired and bind the edges.

Appendix A

Sample Design Work Sheets

Make several photocopies of the following pages so you can sketch layouts and make notes on interesting Strips That Sizzle block arrangements you may develop.

The larger squares are useful for sketching actual block configurations. You may want to cut the photocopied pages in half; in your idea book, glue the grid down on one side of the sheet, with room to the right of it to glue down a snapshot of "real blocks" that have been arranged in the block configuration sketched on the grid.

The smaller squares are handy for planning light strategies by shading in squares to indicate dark Strips That Sizzle blocks; leave squares blank to represent the light ones.

Appendix B

Multi-fabric Border Units

Although sewing Strips That Sizzle quilts does not require templates, it is easier to complete some border designs in the quilts that appear in this book by using a few templates. To make the templates required, you will need:

graph paper (large sheets)
poster board
spray adhesive or rubber cement
ruler, pencils, eraser
rotary cutters, one for fabric and one for paper
acrylic ruler, rotary cutting surface

To complete the quilts, you will need pencils to draw around the templates onto the fabric, a sewing machine, and pressing equipment.

Making Templates

I will use an illustration of the border on my quilt "Columns" (page 64) to demonstrate how to draft full-size templates for the border pieces. The procedure is the same for any quilt you might design requiring border units to complete diagonally set rows.

1. On graph paper, draw a *full-size* corner of the quilt you are making and assign a number to each template needed to assemble the border.

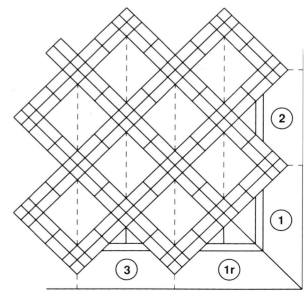

Corner from "Columns"

2. Adhere the graph paper to poster board, using spray adhesive or rubber cement. Cut out templates, using a rotary cutter. At edges of template, make small slashes to mark the position of seam lines in the adjoining units. Use these slashes for matching purposes when attaching border units to the appropriate rows.

3. To use templates, turn them face down on the wrong side of the fabric and trace around them with a sharp pencil. The traced line will be the stitching line.

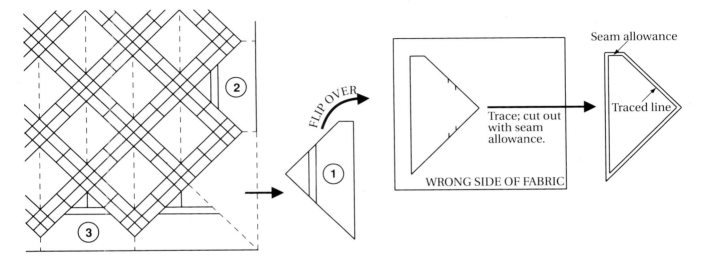

4. Add ¼"-wide seam allowances all around before cutting.

Note: Marking the templates onto the fabric in this way makes it easy to pin the pieces together and match the stitching lines for accurate piecing. Although this is the procedure normally used for hand piecing, it can be used for machine piecing as well.

Cutting Multi-fabric Border Units

When borders require units of several colors, I strip piece the required fabrics together in the required widths ahead of time, and I make a "multiple template" with slashes in the edges to mark the seam-line positions. That way, I can cut the required border piece from the assembled strips of fabric as one unit rather than cutting separate templates for each piece in the unit.

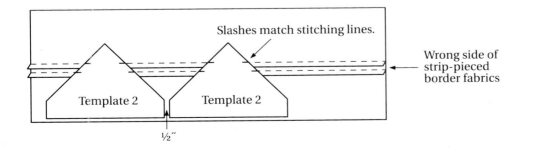

Some border units may be composed of one-half of a Strips That Sizzle strip-pieced block, as is template 3 in the example. You can use a "multiple template" for this border unit, too.

1. Cut Strips That Sizzle block in half, corner to corner, perpendicular to seam line.

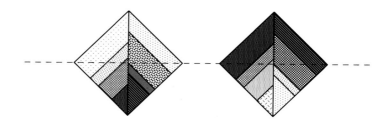

2. Strip piece the remaining fabrics in the required widths and sew the required number of strip-pieced half triangles to the strip.

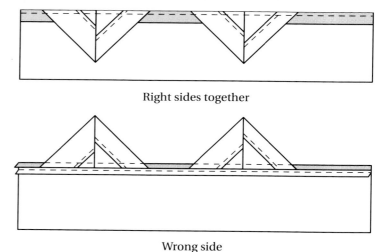

Right sides together

Wrong side

3. Use your "multiple template" to cut the required border unit.

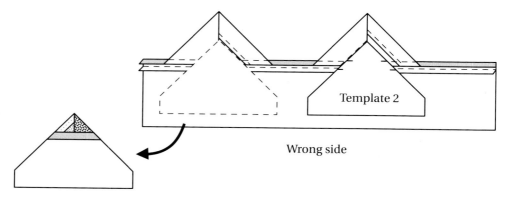

Template 2

Wrong side

Right side

Bibliography

Cox, Patricia. *The Log Cabin Workbook.* 2nd ed. Minneapolis, Minn.: One of a Kind Quilting Designs, 1980.

Dudley, Taimi. *Strip Patchwork.* New York: Van Nostrand Reinhold, 1980.

Itten, Johannes. *The Elements of Color.* ed. Faber Birren. New York: Van Nostrand Reinhold, 1970.

Leman, Bonnie and Judy Martin. *Log Cabin Quilts.* Wheatridge, Colo.: Moon Over the Mountain Publishing Company, 1980.

McKelvey, Susan Richardson. *Color for Quilters.* Atlanta, Ga.: Yours Truly, Inc., 1984.

Orlofsky, Patsy and Myron. *Quilts in America.* New York: McGraw-Hill Book Company, 1974.

Stevens, Peter S. *Handbook of Regular Patterns.* Cambridge, Mass.: The MIT Press, 1981.

Wittman, Lassie. *Seminole Patchwork Patterns.* Rochester, Wash.: self-published, 1979.

Afterword

Quiltmakers can find many heroes among artists from other media— paint, sculpture, clay, fiber, or the written word. One of my heroes is Robert Bateman, the Canadian naturalist, conservationist, and wildlife artist.

During a television program, which the Canadian Broadcasting Company produced on his life and work, Mr. Bateman referred to a master teacher who was a strong influence on him early in his art career. The teacher said that "in order to learn how to draw, you must make at least 2000 mistakes; now get busy and start making them!"

This is a philosophy that serves us well as we learn how to use color in quilts; we can organize fabric and agonize about color choices all day, but until we put one bit of fabric color next to another one, we will never really be able to predict exactly what is going to happen. My fondest wish for you, dear reader, is that you spend many delightful hours working with your fabrics and the exercises in this book. Just jump in, put fabric colors together day in and day out, and enjoy the surprise and joy as well as the expertise that you will surely develop!

Information on lectures and workshops by the author can be obtained by writing to her at:

That Patchwork Place, Inc.
P. O. Box 118
Bothell, Washington 98041

Margaret J. Miller *is a professional quiltmaker, internationally known for her lectures and workshops on color and design that inspire students to "reach for the unexpected" in contemporary quiltmaking. In 1978, while on the faculty of the home economics department at California Polytechnic State University, San Luis Obispo, Margaret learned to quilt and appliqué. It was a natural progression from her lifelong interest in needlework. After a move to San Diego, Margaret started her own business, "Tanglethread Junction," specializing in appliqué and stained-glass appliqué designs. She sold her business in 1982 after making the commitment to become a full-time quiltmaker.*

Margaret's exuberant quilts are displayed and sold through galleries and art consultants. Her teaching schedule has taken her throughout the United States, as well as to Australia and New Zealand. Students love her enthusiasm, infectious humor and sincere encouragement to quiltmakers of all skill levels.

Margaret lives near Seattle, Washington, with her husband and two teenaged sons. If you visit her studio (once the formal living room of her home), you'll find her accompanied by a dog named Puppy and a cat named Trouble.

That Patchwork Place Publications and Products

The *Americana Collection*
by Nancy Southerland-Holmes
Liberty Eagle
Old Glory
Stars and Stripes
Uncle Sam
Angelsong by Joan Vibert
Angle Antics by Mary Hickey
Appliqué Borders: An Added Grace by Jeana Kimball
Baby Quilts from Grandma by Carolann M. Palmer
Back to Square One by Nancy J. Martin
Baltimore Bouquets by Mimi Dietrich
A Banner Year by Nancy J. Martin
Basket Garden by Mary Hickey
Blockbuster Quilts by Margaret J. Miller
Calendar Quilts by Joan Hanson
Cathedral Window: A Fresh Look by Nancy J. Martin
Copy Art for Quilters by Nancy J. Martin
Corners in the Cabin by Paulette Peters
Country Threads by Connie Tesene and Mary Tendall
Even More by Trudie Hughes
Fantasy Flowers: Pieced Flowers for Quilters
by Doreen Cronkite Burbank
Feathered Star Sampler by Marsha McCloskey
Fit To Be Tied by Judy Hopkins
*Five- and Seven-Patch Blocks & Quilts for the
ScrapSaver*™ by Judy Hopkins
Four-Patch Blocks & Quilts for the ScrapSaver™
by Judy Hopkins
Handmade Quilts by Mimi Dietrich
Happy Endings—Finishing the Edges of Your Quilt
by Mimi Dietrich
Holiday Happenings by Christal Carter
Home for Christmas by Nancy J. Martin and
Sharon Stanley
In The Beginning by Sharon Evans Yenter
Lessons in Machine Piecing by Marsha McCloskey
Little By Little: Quilts in Miniature by Mary Hickey
More Template-Free™ *Quiltmaking* by Trudie Hughes
My Mother's Quilts: Designs from the Thirties
by Sara Nephew
Nifty Ninepatches by Carolann M. Palmer
Nine-Patch Blocks & Quilts for the ScrapSaver™
by Judy Hopkins

Not Just Quilts by Jo Parrott
Ocean Waves by Marsha McCloskey and Nancy J. Martin
One-of-a-Kind Quilts by Judy Hopkins
On to Square Two by Marsha McCloskey
Painless Borders by Sally Schneider
Pineapple Passion by Nancy Smith and Lynda Milligan
A Pioneer Doll and Her Quilts by Mary Hickey
Pioneer Storybook Quilts by Mary Hickey
Quilts to Share by Janet Kime
Red and Green: An Appliqué Tradition by Jeana Kimball
Reflections of Baltimore by Jeana Kimball
Rotary Riot: 40 Fast and Fabulous Quilts by Judy Hopkins
and Nancy J. Martin
Scrap Happy by Sally Schneider
Shortcuts: A Concise Guide to Metric Rotary Cutting
by Donna Lynn Thomas
Shortcuts: A Concise Guide to Rotary Cutting
by Donna Lynn Thomas
Small Talk by Donna Lynn Thomas
Stars and Stepping Stones by Marsha McCloskey
Tea Party Time: Romantic Quilts and Tasty Tidbits
by Nancy J. Martin
Template-Free™ *Quiltmaking* by Trudie Hughes
Template-Free™ *Quilts and Borders* by Trudie Hughes
Threads of Time by Nancy J. Martin
Women and Their Quilts by Nancyann Johanson Twelker

Tools
6" Bias Square®
8" Bias Square®
Metric Bias Square®
BiRangle™
Pineapple Rule
Rotary Mate™
Rotary Rule™
ScrapSaver™

Video
Shortcuts to America's
Best-Loved Quilts

Many titles are available at your local quilt shop. For more information, send $2 for a color catalog to That Patchwork Place, Inc., PO Box 118, Bothell WA 98041-0118.